MIKAEL EINARSSON
& HUBBE LEMON

THE
WILD GAME
COOKBOOK

Simple Recipes for
Hunters and Gourmets

gestalten

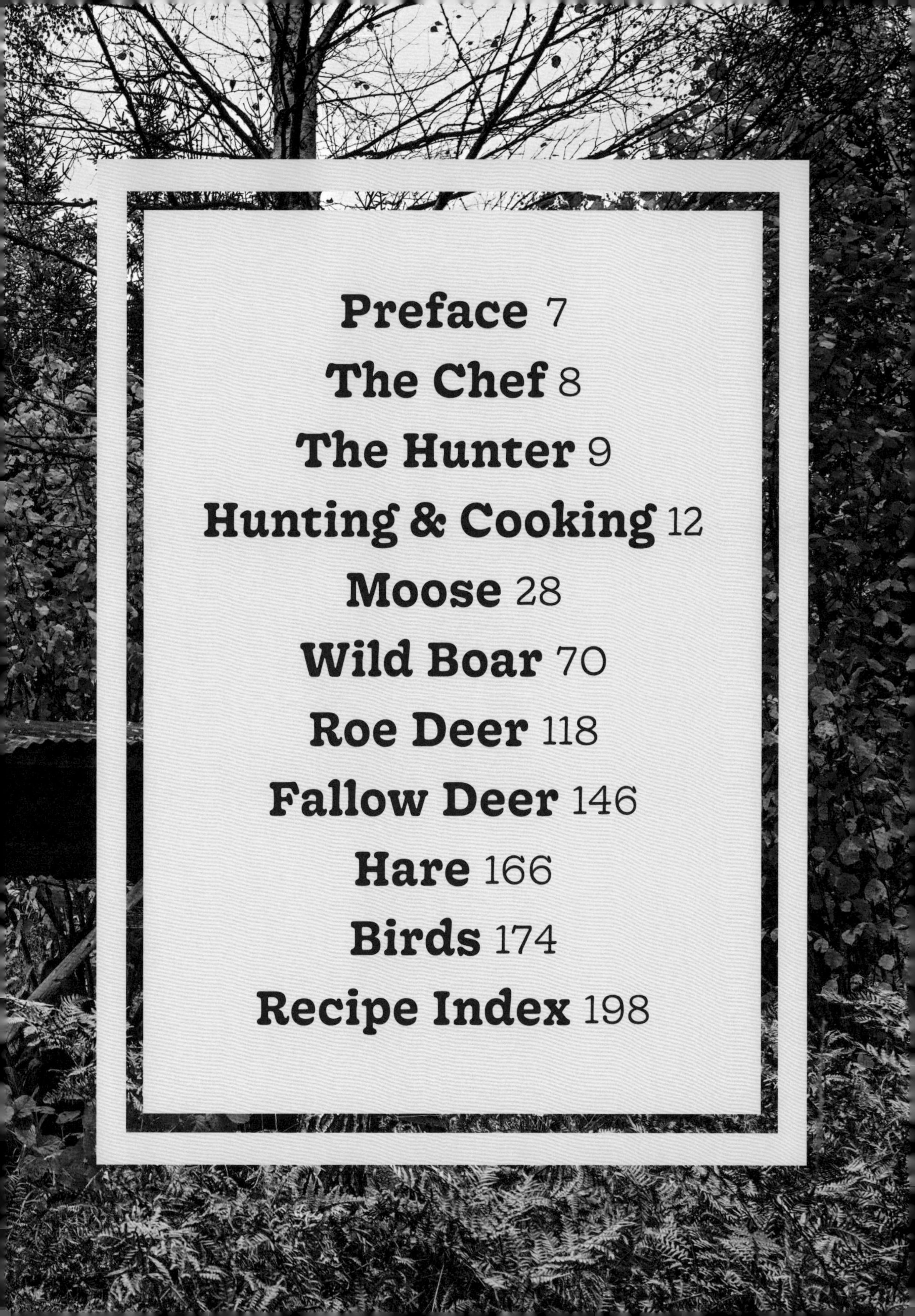

Preface

I t isn't easy to say what it is about hunting that makes it so special. Perhaps it's a cliché, but there's something primal and authentic about hunting—seeking out, killing, and cooking a wild animal. But the fact that it feels primal doesn't necessarily mean it's barbaric or uncivilized. Quite the opposite. Hunting requires organization, discipline, self-awareness, and a lot of knowledge—together with an ethical discussion that's constantly ongoing in your head. Hunting is euphoria and a racing heart, stillness and patience, silence and explosions.

It's easy for two hunters to understand each other. You don't need to explain to another hunter why you'll voluntarily get up at stupid o'clock to sit for hours, still as a statue and silent as the grave, in an isolated hunting tower with the rain whipping into your face and icicles for toes. Why, dressed in a white coverall, you can ski for hours over broken snow crust and burst into a huge smile when a capercaillie disappears over the treetops. Why you don't leap back when your hunting buddy slices a hanging buck from belly to neck and lets gravity do the work of removing the innards and organs. Maybe it's a question of how close to nature you want to be. For some, hunting is too extreme. For us, it adds a value that we struggle to find anywhere else.

It's probably the contrast the hunter seeks. Searching for movement at the forest's edge against searching for a free parking space in the chaos outside the mall. Replacing the grinding noises of the subway with the crackling of birch bark on the fire.

If you're already a hunter, my aim with this book is to spark an interest in cooking really good wild game. Maybe nobody ever said, "The better the chef, the better the hunter," but we think it's true all the same. If you do everything to make sure the final dish is as good as possible, you'll also make sure you shoot really well. Learning more about cooking game means less wild-caught meat ends up becoming ground meat for lack of inspiration.

If you feel you can get something enjoyable from every aspect of the hunt—the preparations, the practice, the hunting itself, and preparing and cooking the animal—then hunting is truly something for you, and you have a lifetime of community, fantastic experiences out in nature, and great meals ahead of you.

—Mikael & Hubbe

The Chef

When I take the electric bike to Brasserie Astoria at Nybrogatan 15 in Stockholm every morning, it's with the knowledge that battle awaits in just two hours. More than 40 chefs work in my kitchen, and as head chef I make sure everything goes according to plan. The five sous-chefs, and the station chefs for hot dishes, cold dishes, the grill, desserts, shellfish, the terrace, and the prep kitchen. When the order tickets are coming in thick and fast, the job is at its most fun but also toughest. A place like Astoria should pulsate. It's the beating heart of the city, and the instant we open there's no going back. I stand with the sous-chefs at the pass and plate up dish after dish. Hundreds of guests with high expectations must be satisfied in the dining rooms every day.

I was born in Gränna in southern Sweden and knew I was going to be a chef from an early age. After studying economics in college and then working in the restaurant business for a year, I went all out to become a chef. My early workplaces include Aspa Herrgård, Norrlands Bar & Grill, Restaurang Kattegatt, and Pontus in the Greenhouse. Then I moved to London and spent a year at two-Michelin-starred The Square. After a few more stops in Stockholm, I took the chance to become head chef at Skebo Herrgård. What appealed was the connection with Järinge Farm, near Hallstavik, not far from Stockholm, which offered wild game in addition to raising and slaughtering animals. This was also where I met Hubbe for the first time. I don't remember the exact occasion, but in all probability he came screeching into the courtyard of the manor house with a couple of mallards in a box or a hare in the trunk of the car. He took me hunting, including for wild boar, and inspired me to eventually take the hunters' exam myself.

My career as a chef continued at the Djuret restaurant in Stockholm, where we made it a point of honor to use one animal at a time and to work conscientiously with all the different cuts. Game meat was used in a variety of ways, including in the pre-rigor mortis dinner that we organized with Äleby Farm, near Stallarholmen, Södermanland. A fallow deer was shot, and we butchered and prepared the still-warm body, in front of the guests, one cut at a time. That may sound macho and brutal, but it was all about showing how we'd actually killed an animal, and emphasizing the responsibility we felt to use it in the best possible way.

When Astoria closes for the night, I bike back to my family. If I'm lucky, I have time for a little hunting on the weekend. Me, Hubbe, the dogs, and the forest. It's as far from the bustle of the restaurant as you can get. But there's still a connection.

—Mikael

The Hunter

As a child we had 13 dogs, and every Saturday morning we had to get up at five o'clock because one of the dogs was going to the hunt. I hated those mornings. I was born and raised in Söderhamn in central Sweden, and because both my mother and father hunted, my entire childhood was tied up with hunting. I always went with them into the forest.

That made me rebellious about hunting, of course, and as a teenager my biggest interest was fishing, even though hunting was never far away. I did pretty much nothing but fish up to the age of 20, and after attending agricultural college in Älvdalen, I became a fishing guide and worked at a camp near Arjeplog in the north of the country. While I was there I guided a man named Rickard, who turned out to be the owner of Järinge Farm. He wondered if I'd be interested in moving there and managing hunting on the estate. I was, and 20 years later I'm still there. We have around 3,200 acres (1,300 ha) of land, organic farming, and hunting for ducks, pheasants, moose, hare, roe deer, and wild boar. We also have a large fallow deer herd of 300–400 animals. I live on the farm with my two children, my girlfriend, and the dogs. I have a German Shorthaired Pointer, Mirja, whom I primarily hunt ptarmigan and forest birds with, and a hunting retriever, Aria, who does a great job of retrieving. We also have Ester, a Chihuahua, Shih Tzu, and Papillon cross, who's actually a pet but who's picked up a lot from our hunting dogs. I sometimes use her to search for wounded animals and for mink hunting.

Working with hunting involves many different tasks. There are stands to clear and maintain (we have more than 100 stands on the estate's land), salt licks to lay out, and game meadows to be cultivated. This means the area becomes attractive for game. We might sow sunflowers in a meadow for the pheasants to peck at the seeds during the winter, or cultivate wild cabbage, which deer love. In some years, we sow some outer areas with peas, and in late summer that attracts a lot of wood pigeons. We might also give certain wild species a boost, by adding to the stock of duck and pheasants to make for better hunting.

Organizing major hunts is also part of the job. That can be likened to arranging a wedding. The planning has to be meticulous—there need to be dog handlers and stand lines for shooters; maps have to be printed and logistics organized, and there's lunch to be served in the forest… plus the game that's been shot needs to be dealt with. Creating a good hunt requires rigorous attention to detail. The focus is always on shooting the right animal in the right way and then handling the kill correctly. It's harder work than you'd think, and it mustn't turn out like *The High Chaparral* in the forest—the hunters need to shoot well and cleanly and come home with good ingredients.

9

When I hunt, the big hunts don't appeal. I enjoy stalking—in other words, tracking game in the forest—or hunting with a friend and our dogs in the mountains. For me, the most enjoyable bit is no longer the shooting itself. I used to think the number of animals was the only way to measure how good a hunter I was, but now it's as least as rewarding to introduce someone else to hunting. Helping someone else to shoot their first roe deer is a fantastic feeling.

When I hunt, my thoughts go quiet. It doesn't matter if it's snowing or there's a howling wind, when you're walking along with the dog bounding out in front of you and your rifle over your shoulder, you're just there, walking. I might stalk a buck or wait at a blind to protect the growing shoots from grubbing wild boar snouts. I hunt grouse and capercaillie on skis, and seabirds in the Stockholm Archipelago. I walk miles in the forest, get physically tired, and fall asleep happy. Now I'm happy to go out hunting without firing a single shot. Once you've fired your rifle, you've got at least a few hours' work ahead of you.

When I walk in the forest, animals are never far away. I can see the rubs on the tree trunks from the bucks rubbing their antlers, which show that I'm inside the roe buck's territory. Or perhaps there are teeth marks on the trunks from a big boar. Observing things like where the boar shelter can be useful to make sure they stay in the forest instead of straying into the fields. For me, hunting, nature, the forest, and farming go together. Hunting has helped me get to know animal behavior, movement patterns, how they seek out food, and whether there are predators in the vicinity.

My basic approach is that you don't shoot loads of animals you aren't prepared to eat. I've hunted with many people who don't want to watch the butchery, who think it's disgusting. And I think they've taken up the wrong hobby. This isn't a sport like tennis or basketball. You're shooting animals. Hunting is what it is, and you can't escape any part of that. Many people think you can just pay your way out of everything, but then you're missing the holistic approach, the feeling that you've done everything, from shot to plate, which makes it really feel genuine and authentic.

—Hubbe

HUNTING &
COOKING

Hunting means different things to different people, but when we talk about hunting the starting point is classic hunting to support your family. And apart from game management, that involves killing an animal to utilize it and cook it, just like country people always used to. Everything else is secondary. We see it neither as a sport nor as a purely social phenomenon, even though, of course, hunting is both exciting and a great way to socialize.

The first step on the path to the forest is likely to be completing a hunter education course, which could cover game species, game management, knowledge of weapons, shooting and hunting legislation, and also perhaps a number of practical tests depending on which type of weapon you want to use (i. e. shotgun or rifle) as well as a big game test using a rifle. There may not be an age limit for the course, but you must have the physical capabilities required for weapon management to do the practical tests. To apply for a license for a hunting weapon, you must usually be at least 18.

A question everyone asks after taking a course is "How can I actually get out and hunt?" Unfortunately, it's not as easy as just heading out into the forest. Getting into a hunting association from the outset isn't a given, and not everyone has a contact network that can help. Our advice is quite simply to talk about hunting with everyone you meet. Talk to landowners—perhaps they need help with shooting wild boar? And, of course, you can also pay to shoot as a guest of a company that organizes hunts. See these occasions as opportunities to make contacts with other hunters. It can also be useful to join this type of arranged hunt to get hunting experience under organized conditions.

Weapons

Nowadays, it is normally possible to buy a rifle which will suit your budget, but remember that both the cheap and expensive weapons fire straight over 260 ft. (80 m), which is the distance you're mainly going to be shooting over. So, I don't think you should overthink the impact of the weapon. How you shoot is almost entirely about your own skill.

For many people, hunting seems to be all about the gear. Apparently, everyone now needs a linear reloading rifle, for instance, but I see that as mainly a fashion. My favorite rifle dates from 1979, and is a Carl Gustaf 1900. I shoot well with it, and I don't see any reason to replace it.

As a new hunter, you probably have lots of questions about which may be the right weapon for you. My advice is to go to a good gun store and try out the weapons. The salesperson will be able to help you find a rifle that works well with your body, with a long enough stock and the right height comb so it sits correctly against your cheek. This will give you the right conditions for a good shot.

To get into hunting seriously, all you really need to begin with is two different rifles: a Class 1 rifle and a shotgun.

You can use a good used shotgun your entire life if you look after it well. In terms of a rifle, you can buy a standard rifle, and invest in a telescopic sight. The scope can be expensive in this context. My advice is to spend a bit more on the glass and a bit less on the shotgun than you'd intended.

If you want to expand your arsenal, I'd recommend a .22 Long Rifle, which is good to practice with and the ammunition doesn't cost much. It's a bit over the top to go out with a Class 1 hunting rifle to shoot targets. With a shotgun, a Class 1 hunting rifle, and a .22 Long Rifle, you can go a long way. And then your specific hunting interest may lead you to buying a Class 2 rifle, a slightly lighter bird gun, or something else.

If you have a dog that drives both hare and roe deer, you can choose a combination rifle/shotgun with barrel selector, which shoots both bullets and shot. A drilling is a heavy version of this, firing two shotgun slugs and one bullet. These have become popular among roe deer hunters, because, if you happen to encounter a legal wild boar, you can take that with the bullet.

I think that even after passing your hunters' exam you should be active with your shooting. Go to the shooting range a few times a year so you know you're going to shoot well on the day you're aiming at an animal. If you think the recoil is unpleasant, and it means you tense up, you can install a silencer. This removes a lot of the recoil and can also help you with target shooting because it helps keep the weapon steady. Remember that a light rifle "kicks" more than a heavy one.

A concise hunting glossary

at bay—when an animal being driven forward turns back.
beater—a person who walks through the forest making a noise to drive the game toward the shooters.
birdy—when a dog gets excited as it strikes a fresh scent.
covert (with a silent *t*)—a small area of gamebird habitat.
dispatch—to kill a wounded animal.
dressing the animal—removing the innards and organs of the game.
leading—when firing at moving game, the weapon is aimed slightly ahead to hit the target.
rut—the fall breeding season for cervids (deer).
scope—the telescopic sight mounted on a hunting rifle.
slob hunter—a hunter who disregards game laws or who otherwise acts inconsiderately.
stand—the area where hunting will take place.
swing—to aim the weapon in a sweeping movement towards moving game before firing.

Types of hunting

You can hunt with a shotgun or a rifle, with or without a dog, alone or as part of a hunting association. Here are the most common types of hunting in Sweden:

Drive hunting

Drive hunting is one of the most common forms of hunting in Sweden. The shooters wait at a stand, often in a hunting tower that gives a good view and firing angle. The animals are driven across the stand by beaters and dog handlers in a beating line. During a drive hunt there can be a lot of people moving in the forest, and a number of shooters, and making sure everyone stays safe requires good organization. Many different types of game can be hunted with a drive hunt—both small and larger animals. The distances to the animals are often short.

Hunting hare with a dog has always been perceived something only old men do, but it's a type of hunting I really appreciate. It's just you, your dog, and a flask of coffee. A hound is a long-legged dog that you only use for hunting foxes and hare. You see the hare run past three or four times over a couple of hours, and finally you may fire a shot.

Stalking

Stalking means that you sneak after game rather than flushing it out. This can be done in different ways. Either you go and sit in a tower and simply wait for the game to come to you, which requires great patience and good padding on your backside. Of if you want to make it more difficult, you try to sneak up on the game. When you spot an animal, you can remove your shoes and creep along in your socks to make as little noise as possible. When stalking, the most important thing—apart from moving silently—is to keep track of the wind direction. If you fail to do this, you won't succeed because the game will detect your scent from a long way off.

Blind hunting

Blind hunting involves you waiting for the game—often wild boar—at a feeding site. Because this hunting method mostly involves waiting, and because the game generally stands still as you take aim, I feel this is a little less exciting. It's simply too easy, and the period before the shot isn't as exciting if you're an experienced hunter.

Regardless of the type of hunting, a search of the site is carried out directly after shooting to give an indication of how the animal was shot. Here we can see fresh blood on the leaves.

Hunting with a bay dog

This is a hunting method where the dog runs in front of the game, or close on the animal's heels, so that it stops to confront the dog. The dog stands and barks at the animal—this is known as "baying." As the hunter, you then try to get within range, which involves making sure you stay downwind, so the animal doesn't get your scent. When the dog barks, you move. When it's quiet, you stay still. Baying allows the hunter a chance to catch up, because the game is still, and it's also a distraction from the presence of the hunter. This offers a good chance of dropping the quarry without too much stress.

Hunting with a pointing dog

With bird dogs such as pointers, you can try out another form of hunting, which is often used for birds such as ptarmigan, capercaillie, grouse, quail, or pheasant. The dog marks where the bird is by standing still and pointing with its muzzle. Then the hunter walks up to the dog, loads the rifle and then commands the dog to flush the bird—in other words, to move forward directly at the bird and to make it fly into the air. The dog should immediately lie down so the hunter can safely swing and shoot at the bird. This can be very difficult for the dog to learn, and requires a great deal of training.

Hunting with a short-distance dog

These dogs have a short range, perhaps only 15 minutes. The shooters sit in a U-shaped arrangement around the stand and the dog handlers walk toward the firing line. The dogs disturb game in the area, such as roe deer, which they drive for 15 minutes before running back to their handlers. Then they seek out another animal and drive it forward.

Hunting with a retriever

If you're going to hunt seabirds, you need a retriever—a dog that will swim out and fetch the quarry. Many breeds can be used, and you can also use a retriever for hunting animals on land.

Hunting with barking bird-dogs

This is another form of hunting for birds, often using spitz-type dogs such as the Finnish Spitz. The dog runs through the forest and seeks out a capercaillie, for instance. The capercaillie flies into a tree and perches. Then the dog stands beneath the tree and barks, and the hunter can creep into range and fire.

Hunting with terriers

Working with dogs that pursue foxes and badgers underground into their dens or setts. The legality of this practice should be checked in your local jurisdiction.

Wounded animals

If you shoot an animal and it doesn't die within 330 ft. (100 m) of the place it was hit, you are required to suspend the hunt and call in search dogs. Most often, you'll soon find the dead animal. But when things have gone so wrong that, for example, you've hit a front leg or shot the deer in the gut, then you have to hunt and shoot the deer once more. During the search, there's never a good firing position, because as soon as the animal is wounded it will seek out the most inaccessible place it can find—far into the brushwood, marsh, or undergrowth, or in the reeds by a watercourse.

It isn't nice to be the one who's got it wrong when hunting, and the shame you feel after a bad shot is a heavy burden. No hunter wants to be the person who's wounded an animal, so think carefully about what you're doing. Don't get stressed about trying to shoot more than one animal at a go. Focusing on one at a time is always best.

After the shot

In the same second that you fire, you should try to remember where the animal was standing when the shot went off—for example, "right by the big birch." Also take note of where it moves from that point. Exactly where does it disappear into the trees? This gives you point A and point B so you can carefully search the area. Between these two points you should find blood and hair and perhaps lung residues from the shot.

Drag the animal out if it's lying partly in bushes or scrub. If you're going to dress the animal in the forest, first make sure you won't need to drag the animal through a marsh or something before you open it up. You need to keep it as clean as possible. Let's take the moose, as in the images opposite, as our example: First make a cut along the neck up to the chin so you can release the esophagus and trachea. Cut the trachea, then cut the esophagus and tie a knot in it. If you seal it with a cable tie or similar, make sure you don't leave it behind in the forest.

Next, you open the stomach, from groin to breastbone, and remove the rectum, bladder, and genitals. You can tie a knot in the rectum, to avoid getting feces outside the intestines. I usually carry this step out after I get to the slaughterhouse. Remove the intestines, stomach, and all the other organs. If you want to set aside the heart and kidneys, do that now.

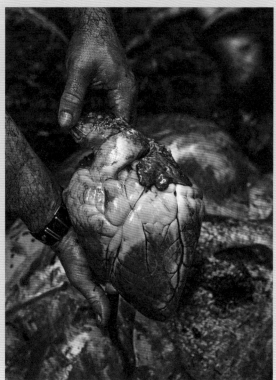

The shot that killed this moose went straight through the lungs, so the heart is completely intact.

If it's a smaller animal such as a roe deer, hang it up from the hindquarters and skin it. It's always easier to remove the skin when the animal is still warm. Now you should cut around each hind leg, but don't cut from outside in. Instead, stick the knife in under the skin and cut from inside out. Otherwise, you'll cut off loads of tiny hairs from the skin and they'll scatter everywhere—and you don't want them on the meat. Then you can pull the skin down and remove it from the rest of the animal. Saw off the hoofs, and head and allow the body to hang for an appropriate length of time depending on the temperature.

Butchering a roe deer.
Top left: Remove the
front shoulder block. Top
right: Remove the loins.
Opposite page, clockwise
from top left: Remove
the tenderloin; cut out the
loins; some parts of the
butchered animal (steaks,
neck, loin, and tenderloin);
remove the pelvis.

There are many videos online that can teach you how to
butcher game, but here are the essentials for a roe deer:

1. Cut off the two front shoulder blocks.
2. Cut the neck away from the ribcage.
3. Saw through the breastbone.
4. Saw off the ribs on each side so you get a whole slab of ribs
   with meat in between.
5. Make a cut where the ribs begin and the saddle ends.
   Make a cut toward the spine. Saw so that you end up with
   the rack end of the saddle with the entrecote and a bit
   of the striploin, while the fillets remain on the saddle.
6. Cut off the fillets so they remain on the saddle.
   Make a cut in the back and remove the entire saddle.
7. Now you have the hindquarters with the pelvic bone
   in the middle. Remove the upper parts of the fillet that
   remain in the groin.
8. Divide the pelvic bone in two or cut around it if you don't
   want to keep it attached.

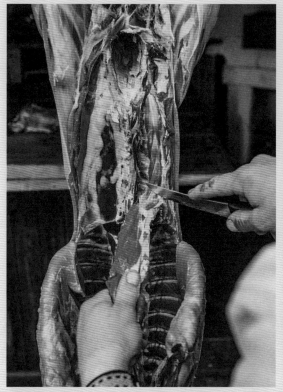

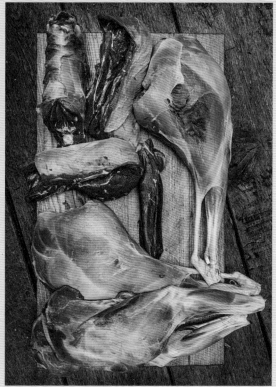

Cooking

I encourage all hunters to take as much of an interest in cooking as possible. There are a number of "obvious" things that many hunters do which I feel are a bit unnecessary, such as reflexively putting all newly shot meat into the freezer as soon as you get it home. If you shoot a roe deer at the start of the hunting season in late August, why freeze it all? It's very shortsighted. Enjoy fresh game meat as often as you can!

Don't see limitations with wild game. It feels like the fear of doing the wrong thing is bigger when it comes to game than with other meat. But don't be afraid of what goes together—or not. It's your own taste that's important. If you want to do a nice bit of roe venison with homemade fries and Béarnaise sauce, why not? Of course, there's nothing wrong with the classic recipes, such as seasoning with thyme and juniper berries and making a good cream sauce, but it's not the only thing you can do either.

Remember that you can make stock with the bones, and learn to cook recipes where the meat stays on the bone. That makes it a whole different thing, and the meat develops a richer flavor. And perhaps most important of all, make sure you keep whole parts other than the loin. It's such a shame if everything ends up as ground meat.

Techniques

When it comes to techniques, I think you should use more advanced kitchen equipment with caution. For example, using the sous-vide technique to cook lean, tender fillets of game tends not to be a great idea, as the meat can easily develop a pâté-like texture. It's better to fry it quickly over a high heat to get a good color and then finish it in the oven at a slightly higher temperature. Instead, you can use sous-vide to slow-cook neck or shoulder with garlic, olive oil, and spices. If you cook it overnight at not too low a temperature, it turns out beautifully. Remember that lean meat is best fried in lots of butter.

Wild flavors

I usually start with whatever the animal ate in the season when it was shot. For example, roe deer are really picky connoisseurs and eat extremely specific herbs with a lot of flavor. And that comes out in the meat, too. If I shoot a roe deer at the end of August or early September, I cook the saddle fresh, with the same type of herbs that I think it might have eaten, and supplement those with fresh green beans and the first mushrooms of the season.

Fallow deer are perhaps the least discerning animal when it comes to fodder, which largely consists of grass. The meat tastes good, but maybe not as special as that of a roe deer.

What I cook using moose primarily depends on how big the animal was. The meat of a moose calf is light, lean, and delicate; that of a cow can be greasier with a wonderful texture, while the meat of a bull moose can be both lean and muscular. In November, I naturally serve them with root vegetables.

I notice recipes for wild boar are in demand, and there seems to be some uncertainty about what to cook. As an example, we've made great bacon from really fatty wild boar, even though the majority of wild boar are too lean. And, of course, we could make more wild boar sausage, or make it more often.

It's always nicest to cook birds with the skin on, but to be honest it's a real job to pluck a dozen or so birds if you've had a successful hunt, and nor is it easy to keep the skin whole. It's much quicker to just remove the breasts, but if you have time it's worth having a go at plucking them. Particularly with ducks, which often have greasier skin, it makes a big difference if you can cook them with the skin on. Wild duck legs are also good, and you can generally approach them as if they were domestic ducks. Don't forget to make stock with the carcass.

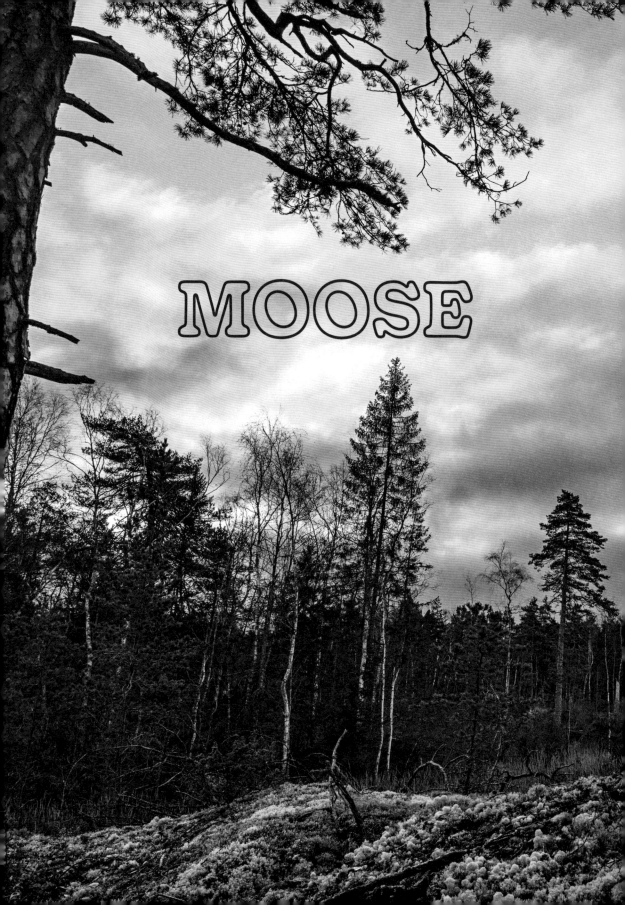

MOOSE

A day's hunting on Järinge Farm begins with a briefing.

The second Monday in October, when moose hunting begins in southern Sweden, is always a big day for me. I fill my vacuum flask and check the radio equipment is charged. The hunting group meets early in the morning, and despite the animated atmosphere, safety and order are the keywords. It's my task as the hunt leader to make sure everyone in the group understands the rules. When you hunt with a rifle, there's an almost military precision—you need to keep a close eye on your rifle, the bolt, and your ammunition. After the hunt, it's OK to feel a little elation, but not before.

We go through radio communication, how you report, and general safety rules. Everyone should already know them, but it doesn't hurt to have a reminder of the most important aspects: There must be solid ground behind the game when you fire. When the bullet has gone through the animal, it must go into the earth, not be able to continue and risk hitting someone. The forest doesn't offer solid ground, so you never fire at an animal that's broadside on. Trees don't make good backstops. The hunting tower means you're shooting from a higher position than the animal, and so the direction of fire is downward.

Finally, I present the dog handlers and dogs and explain how they will work. Every hunter gets a map with a few drives marked

on it, and the group climbs into the vehicles, which take everyone out to the stands. When I started hunting, the instruction might have been something like "You're by the tall pine," but now we work in a more controlled way so everyone knows where everyone else is, at clearly named stands. When everyone's in place at their stand in the forest, the shooters get the go-ahead to load their weapons, and I signal to the dog handlers and the beating line.

And so begins the hunt. As hunt leader, my hope is always that you'll get to see lots of game, because that shows I've managed the game and planning well and arranged good dog handlers. Of course, whether the hunt is a success is up to the shooters.

As a shooter, your first thought when an animal appears should be a quick decision about whether this animal is a designated target. Perhaps we're only shooting calves and bulls on this hunt, so you have to make a decision very fast. If there's a cow and a calf, it's quite easy to immediately distinguish calves that are valid targets, and in that scenario it's difficult to make a mistake even if you're new to hunting. If you need to shoot an adult male, you need to be alert if a cow and then a calf appear—because a bull will often be trailing 50–65 ft. (15–20 m) behind them.

After you've checked that the animal is a valid target, you need a good opportunity to fire—in other words, when the selected moose stops in one of your firing lines or is outlined against a field. Can you fire a sure shot? Will your shot be lethal? You have to be thoughtful but at the same time hungry—if you're too relaxed in this situation, you may not fire in time. When everything feels right, you fire. The bullet travels straight because, of course, you've test-fired the weapon earlier. You hit the target, and you see how the moose perhaps begins to limp and walk in a tight curve. It disappears into the forest, but you hear a thump and then there's a lot of rustling in the undergrowth, and then everything goes quiet. This means the animal has lain down, kicked a little, and has now died. After the drama, and after the other animals have fled, you report on the radio to the hunt leader that at stand 6A you've shot a calf. Everything feels right, and you explain that you think the animal fell almost immediately. The hunt leader will order a dog handler to examine the site and then track the animal. As a rule, the dog will immediately find the fallen animal. Depending on whether the animal was stressed and ran before the shot was fired, it may have run a greater or lesser distance after it was hit.

My top tip for succeeding with a moose hunt, apart from a little luck, is to simply be very, very quiet. If you're going to be hunting a drive of 500 acres (200 ha), and there will be 12 shooters arranged in a horseshoe shape around it, everyone will go out into the forest at the same time. Everyone's eager and a little stressed, which leads to a lot of noise in the forest. If you instead move calmly, creeping to your stand and taking five minutes longer to get there and so not allowing the game to hear you, you have a lot more chance that they'll move toward you. The moose will have heard all the hunters around you and will then head for the spot that seems to be the calmest and quietest. So, it's often the person who dawdles in 10 minutes late who gets to shoot first, because they haven't made so much commotion. In other words, it's important that everyone gets to their place in the line, because if there's a hole in the net the game generally spot it. You should also remember that a moose often moves diagonally upwind when hunted by a dog so it knows it won't run into another threat.

Don't worry if the dogs don't start any animals straightaway. Moose can pause in an area of a few hundred square yards for quite a long time. They are patient animals and will keep an eye on the dogs and handlers. They listen and wait for the people making the noise to go away. Only when the forest has fallen silent will they creep away.

You'd think you would hear a moose because they look large and clumsy, but they actually move amazingly quietly, and suddenly there can be one standing there in front of you. Of course, if the

Rub marks on trees indicate there's a bull moose in the area.

moose is being chased by a dog, it may make more noise as it runs through the forest.

If a moose comes along that doesn't have a dog after it, and it's moving at a placid pace, you can try giving a short whistle. This will make the moose stop and look, and it can give you the extra seconds you need to get the crosshairs perfectly aligned behind its shoulders so you can fire calmly.

After a moose has fallen, it should be transported out of the forest. Hopefully, it will be relatively accessible terrain, because otherwise you'll have to drag it out using muscle power alone until you can use a quad, tractor, and so on.

The moose is taken out of the forest and left to hang so the meat becomes tender. Hanging is calculated in "day degrees," and a moose should be hung for 40-60 day degrees, depending on how much fat it has and what time of year it is. In the fall, this is about 7-10 days. It's then butchered, and the different cuts are packaged. The meat is often divided among the hunting group. We hunt from morning until one hour before dusk and then we have dinner, with many hunting stories to accompany it. Then we do the same thing on the following day.

6 things to remember

1. Put your cell phone on silent or leave it in your vehicle.
2. Don't slam car doors when you head out to the stand.
3. Unscrew the lid of your vacuum flask, rather than pressing the button (if it has one), as it makes a loud CLICK!
4. Make sure picnics are rustle-free. Better a lunchbox than plastic bags.
5. Don't pee at the stand—it spreads your scent.
6. Sit ready with your rifle on your knee. Game comes and goes quickly. If your rifle is leaning or lying beside you, 8 out of 10 animals will have run through the stand before you've got it up to your eye.

Moose

When it comes to Swedish hunts, most people probably think of the traditional moose hunt. The moose is the largest wild animal in Sweden, but in the early 1800s it was almost extinct. After hunting began to focus more on young animals instead of older ones, more cows could produce calves, and the species recovered. The population was at its biggest in the 1980s, and since then it has approximately halved.

Biology & ecology

Male: bull
Female: cow
Young: calf

The moose is a ruminant, cloven-hoofed animal with adults weighing up to 1,100 lb. (500 kg) and being more than 6½ ft. (2 m) tall at the shoulder. The color of its coat can vary from almost black to light brown. The bull's antlers can have two different shapes: pole-shaped, which is most common in southern Sweden, and shovel-shaped, which is most common in the north of the country. The size of the antlers signals status, and the bulls shed their antlers annually in the winter.

Moose bulls begin to rut at about 3 years of age. Moose cows produce most calves between 4 and 12 years of age.

The moose primarily eats leaves and woody plants. In the winter, that means twigs from conifers and deciduous trees; in the spring, a lot of berry bushes and heather; and in the summer, the leaves of deciduous trees, low-growing plants, and grass.

Hunting period

North of Lake Siljan: September 1–January 31.
Other parts of Sweden: October 8–January 31.
   Local variations occur. Check with the County Administrative Board where you're going to hunt. Moose may be hunted from an hour before sunrise to an hour after sunset. During the hour after sunset, the hunt may be done as stalking or blind hunting.

Types of hunting

The most common method is hunting with a bay dog, often combined with shooters at allocated stands. The dog gets the scent of the moose and makes it stop by barking at it. This hunting method has a long tradition in Sweden, with dog breeds specially raised for moose hunting.

Dogs

Mainly Norwegian Elkhound and Jämthund (Swedish Elkhound), sometimes Laika, Karelian Bear Dog, Hällefors Elkhound, and White Swedish Elkhound.

Weapons

Only rifles are permitted. Class 1 ammunition (6.5×55 mm Swedish).

Designated targets

The right number of moose must be shot, with a relatively large proportion of calves, because the average age of the population should be quite high. Large, older bulls and cows are required for early rutting and early calves that develop correctly. Large and older moose lead to high reproduction rates.

Preparation
1 hour
Cooking
50 minutes
Makes
12 portions

Filling
3 lb. 5 oz. (1.5 kg) moose meat, ground
2 tbsp. salt
4 eggs
¾ cup + 4 tsp. (200 ml) milk
1 tbsp. marjoram
1 tsp. black pepper
7 tbsp. (100 g) butter
3 tbsp. soy sauce

Rice
1 onion
⅔ cup (130 g) short-grain white rice
1⅔ cups (400 ml) water
1¼ cups (300 ml) milk
1 tbsp. marjoram
1 tsp. salt

Cabbage
1 large white cabbage

Sauce
juice from baking the cabbage rolls
¾ cup + 4 tsp. (200 ml) game stock (see page 80)
4 cups (1 liter) whipping cream
7 tbsp. (100 ml) lingonberry relish
cornstarch, as needed
salt

To serve
boiled potatoes
lingonberry relish

Moose cabbage rolls

Cabbage rolls take time and planning, but when they're done you've got the tastiest dish in the world, and one that's easy to reheat. Served with boiled potatoes and creamy lingonberry sauce, this dish is an absolute classic. And I promise, when it's your turn to organize lunch for your hunting group and you show up with cabbage rolls, you'll be given the best deer stand forever after! This recipe produces 24 cabbage rolls with just over 3 ounces (90 g) of filling per roll, depending on how big the cabbage leaves are.

Rice

Finely chop the onion and place in a saucepan with the rice and water. Cook for a few minutes over a medium heat. Add the milk, marjoram, and salt, and simmer carefully, stirring from time to time, until the rice is completely soft (add more milk or water if necessary). Leave the rice to cool.

Cabbage

Bring water to a boil in a large saucepan. Cut around the root of the cabbage and lift it out like a plug. Then immerse the cabbage in the boiling water with a roasting fork.

After 4–5 minutes, you can lift the cabbage out of the water and start to carefully remove the outer leaves with tongs. Continue cooking the cabbage and remove more leaves after a few more minutes. Spread the leaves out on a work surface where you can add the filling.

Filling

Preheat the convection oven to 440 °F (225 °C). Using a food processor with a mixing blade or a large bowl and wooden spoon, mix the rice with all the filling ingredients, except for the butter and soy sauce. Grease a large ovenproof baking dish with about half of the butter. Form the filling into sausages of just over 3 oz. (90 g) and place them on the cooked cabbage leaves. Roll and fold the cabbage leaves (fold in both edges to the center and roll into a neat package) and place them close together in the greased ovenproof dish. Bake the rolls for approx. 10 minutes. Distribute the rest of the butter in small knobs across the top of the cabbage rolls and add the soy sauce. Bake for another 20 minutes. Remove from the oven at regular intervals and brush with the liquid in the dish. If necessary, turn the dish so the rolls brown evenly. The cabbage rolls are ready when they have an internal temperature of 170 °F (75 °C) and the cabbage is nicely browned—a little more than golden brown.

Sauce

Heat the ingredients in a saucepan over a medium heat for approximately 20 minutes. Taste and thicken with cornstarch to your liking.

To serve

If you don't intend to serve the cabbage rolls immediately, you can easily reheat them in the sauce in an ovenproof baking dish. Serve with boiled potatoes and lingonberry relish.

Preparation
40 minutes
Cooking
2 hours
Makes
15 portions

Goulash
4 lb. 6 oz. (2 kg) moose knuckle, cut into large cubes
6 garlic cloves
4 tbsp. paprika, ground
2 tbsp. salt
1 tbsp. whole caraway seeds
2 tbsp. (15 g) fresh ginger
11 fl. oz. (330 ml) dark beer
6 cups (1.5 liters) game stock (see page 80)
8 ½ cups (2 liters) water
2 red chilis
2 ¼ lb. (1 kg) waxy potatoes
5 red bell peppers
5 onions
7 oz. (200 g) hot-smoked wild boar belly (see page 106) or hot-smoked pork belly
2 ¼ lb. (1 kg) hot-smoked wild boar salsiccia (see page 84)
7 tbsp. (100 ml) rapeseed oil
good bread for serving

Lemon cream
1 lemon
2 cups (500 ml) smetana (sour cream, approx. 24% fat)
2 tbsp. parsley, chopped
2 tsp. salt
black pepper

Hunter's goulash

A flavorful stew that's ready to be heated during the lunch break is always popular. Here's a great recipe for a moose stew that's even tastier made the day before it's served.

Lemon cream

Wash the lemon, grate the zest, and squeeze the juice. Mix all the ingredients in a bowl and season with salt and pepper. Place in the refrigerator until serving time.

Goulash

Fry the moose meat, garlic cloves, and ground paprika in oil in a large saucepan over a high heat. Allow to become golden brown, stirring from time to time.

Add the salt, caraway seeds, chopped ginger, beer, and stock. Bring to the boil. Add water and chili (use whole ones if you want to be able to remove them). Simmer, checking regularly, for approximately 1 hour.

Cut the potatoes into ¾-in.- (2-cm-) thick slices. Rinse and deseed the red pepper, and cut into large pieces. Then peel and roughly cube the onions. Add the potatoes, red pepper, and onion to the pan. Simmer for a further 20 minutes.

Cut the hot-smoked pork belly into ½-in.- (1-cm-) thick strips and the wild boar salsiccia into ¾-in.- (2-cm-) thick slices. Allow the pork belly and sausage to simmer for another 10 minutes. Season the stew with salt and pepper.

Eat immediately or reheat the stew, before serving with lemon cream and hearty bread.

Moose

**Bean soup with
smoked moose heart**

Preparation
20 minutes
Cooking
1 hour, if you already
have a smoked heart
Makes
6–8 portions

Soup
2½ cups (500 g) dried navy
  beans, soaked at room
  temperature for at least
  6 hours
2 onions
1 garlic clove
¾ cup + 4 tsp. (200 ml)
  white wine
1⅔ cups (400 ml) game
  stock (see page 80)
4 cups (1 liter) water
7 tbsp. (100 g) butter
1 tbsp. squeezed lemon juice
3 tbsp. champagne vinegar
1½ tbsp. salt
rapeseed oil

Toppings
2 shallots
3 tbsp. white wine vinegar
1 cup (200 ml) smoked
  moose heart, diced
  (see opposite page)
2 tbsp. flat-leaf parsley,
  chopped
olive oil
salt and black pepper

Bean soup with smoked moose heart

A warming recipe for a tasty soup with smoked moose heart. Works just as well for a dinner party as it does out in the forest.
Using the moose heart is something I highly recommend. The flavor and consistency are excellent, and you can pat yourself on the back for not wasting such a high-quality cut of meat.

Soup

Drain the soaked beans. Peel and finely chop the onion and
garlic. Sweat the onion and garlic in a few drops of rapeseed oil in a saucepan over a medium heat. Add the beans
and white wine, bring to the boil, and then add the stock
and water. Reduce the heat a little and allow to simmer
for approximately 1 hour, stirring from time to time.
Mix the soup in a blender or with an immersion blender.
Add the butter, lemon juice, vinegar, and salt, and blend
one last time so the mixture is smooth. Season and,
if necessary, add a little more stock or water, because
the soup can easily become too thick.

Toppings

Peel and finely chop the shallots and place in a small saucepan
over a medium heat. Pour over the vinegar and bring to the
boil, then remove from the heat. Place the shallots in a bowl
and mix with the other ingredients. Season with salt and
a few turns of freshly ground black pepper.
Arrange the heart directly on the plates if you're eating at
home, or put it in a plastic container with a lid to add to the
soup later if you're eating in the forest.

Preparation
4 hours
Cooking
4 hours
Makes
6–8 portions

Smoked moose heart
1 moose heart (3⅓–4½ lb. / 1.5–2 kg)
grill or smoker
charcoal, briquettes,
   and small pieces or shavings
   of, for example, applewood

Brine
10 cups (2.5 liters) water
1½ tsp. (25 g) iodine-free salt

Smoked
moose heart

You should always make use of the heart if only the lungs were hit when the animal was shot. This recipe uses a moose heart, but of course it works just as well with other game. You simply adjust the cooking time. Smoked heart is perfect in sandwiches or, as here, in a warming soup.

Cut the heart in half and wash it out with cold water. Measure the cold water for the brine and add the salt. Whisk until the salt dissolves. Place the heart in a suitable dish and cover with brine. Place in the refrigerator and allow the heart to brine for at least 4 hours.

If you don't have access to a dedicated smoker, you can smoke it in a kettle grill. Light the grill with half of the charcoal and briquettes. Take advantage of the glowing coals by cooking something else in the meantime.

Remove the heart from the brine and allow to drain in a colander. Wait until the temperature in the grill under the lid is approximately 300 °F (150 °C). Add the wood chips and heart. Smoke for 3–4 hours at approx. 175 °F (80 °C). Leave the heart to cool then store in the refrigerator. Before serving, you'll need to remove the sinews that hold the heart valves together.

51

Preparation
30 minutes
Cooking
30 minutes (except
the rutabaga cream)
Makes
4 portions

Moose liver
approx. 1 ¾ lb. (800 g)
    moose liver
approx. 6 tbsp. (80 g)
    wheat flour
rapeseed oil and butter
salt and black pepper

Rutabaga cream
14 oz. (400 g) rutabaga
7 tbsp. (100 g) brown butter
7 tbsp. (100 ml) water
approx. 2 tsp. salt

Kale & wild boar bacon
7 oz. (200 g) hot-smoked wild
    boar belly (see page 106)
3 ½ oz. (100 g) kale
14 tbsp. (200 g) brown butter
approx. 7 tbsp. (100 ml)
    small capers
approx. 12 large capers
    with stalks
rapeseed oil and butter

Moose liver and bacon

*Offal is a type of meat that can be challenging for some people.
For me and many others, it's just another part of the animal.
Unlike other cuts of meat, offal should be eaten as fresh as pos-
sible. If you aren't going to cook and eat it immediately, freeze it.
If you're a curious beginner when it comes to offal, this recipe is
probably the best place to start.*

Rutabaga cream

Preheat the oven to 350 °F (175 °C). Rinse the rutabaga and place
it in an ovenproof dish, skin on. Bake on the middle rack
for approximately 3 hours. Check if it's soft enough to pierce
with a skewer. Remove from the oven and leave to cool
slightly. Peel then roughly chop the rutabaga into large pieces.
Place in a blender or mixer, add the warm brown butter
and water, and blend into a smooth cream. Season with salt.

Kale & wild boar bacon

Trim the kale and cut it into pieces approximately 2 in. (5 cm)
long. Dice the hot-smoked wild boar belly into ½-in. (1-cm)
cubes. Fry the meat in equal parts butter and oil over a high
heat for approximately 1 minute, until it starts to brown.
Add the kale and reduce the heat to medium. Fry, stirring
from time to time, for a further 1 minute. Add the capers
and remove from the heat. To serve, top the liver with
the warm brown butter, kale, and wild boar bacon. Serve the
rutabaga cream on the side.

Moose liver

Trim any membrane and sinews from the liver. Cut into
½-in.- (1-cm-) thick slices. Dip the liver in flour and fry in
equal parts butter and oil over a high heat. Fry both sides
until golden brown, approximately 1 minute per side, until
the internal temperature is 125 °F (52 °C). Remove the liver
from the pan and allow to rest for a couple of minutes
before serving.

Preparation
40 minutes
Cooking
10 minutes, but the meat should marinate in the brine for at least 2 days
Makes
4 portions

Moose steak
11 oz. (300 g) moose steak
7 tbsp. (100 ml) stout
3½ tbsp. (50 ml) soy sauce
1 garlic clove
4–5 dried green peppercorns
4–5 dried juniper berries

Ginger cream
7 tbsp. (100 ml) crème fraîche
2 tbsp. mayonnaise
1 tsp. gari (pickled ginger), finely chopped

1 tsp. ginger, finely grated
1 tsp. soy sauce
salt and black pepper

Deep-fried Jerusalem artichokes
2 whole heads of solo garlic
¾ cup + 4 tsp. (200 ml) milk
2 Jerusalem artichokes
oil for deep frying
salt

To serve
scallions
butter-fried chanterelles

Stout-marinated moose steak

Here, I've made a carpaccio of stout-marinated moose steak, but it also works well marinated in the same way and instead cubed finely and served as a tartare. If you want to prepare this in advance, you can marinate the meat and freeze it, so you always have some to hand when you want a special meal.

Moose steak

Bring the stout to the boil in a saucepan. Add the soy sauce, 1 lightly crushed clove of garlic, green peppercorns, and juniper berries.

Remove any membrane and sinews from the meat. Place the meat in a freezer bag or vacuum bag and add the cooled brine. Marinate the meat for 2–3 days in the refrigerator. Remove before serving and allow the meat to dry a little on paper towels. Cut into thin slices and arrange on plates.

Accompaniments & serving

Peel and thinly slice the garlic with a mandoline or slice it as thinly as possible with a knife. Leave the garlic to soak in milk in the refrigerator for at least 2 hours. Sieve and leave to drain. Fry in batches in oil at 355 °F (180 °C) until golden brown. Leave to drain on paper towels, then salt.

Reduce the temperature of the frying oil to approximately 320 °F (160 °C). Rinse the Jerusalem artichokes, then slice them thinly with a mandoline or knife and fry until golden brown. Leave to drain on paper towels, then salt.

Mix all the ingredients into a cream in a bowl, then place in the refrigerator until serving.

Trim the scallions, then slice thinly. Fry the chanterelles in butter. Top the meat with the scallions, chanterelles, ginger cream, and the fried Jerusalem artichokes and garlic.

Preparation
30 minutes
Cooking
approx. 18 hours
Makes
6–8 portions

Tjälknöl
approx. 2 ¼ lb. (1 kg) frozen
  roast moose
4 cups (1 liter) water
2 ¾ tbsp. (50 g) salt
3 ½ tbsp. (50 ml) soy sauce
1 tbsp. sugar
1 garlic clove
1 tsp. crushed black pepper
1 tsp. dried thyme

Pickled red onion
2 red onions
¾ cup + 4 tsp. (200 ml) water
7 tbsp. (100 ml) strong
  vinegar, 12%
6 tbsp. (90 g) sugar

Panzanella
8 slices day-old white bread
6 red tomatoes
6 yellow tomatoes
1 cucumber
⅔ cup (150 ml) red wine
  vinegar
⅔ cup (150 ml) olive oil
7 oz. (200 ml) pickled
  red onion (see left)
1–2 bunches green
  asparagus, boiled
8 heads grilled gem lettuce
4 shredded scallions
fresh herbs (e. g. basil,
  chervil, parsley)
salt and black pepper

Roast moose steak *tjälknöl*

Tjälknöl *is frozen moose or other meat roasted at very low temperature—a perfect summer dish if you have a bit of moose left in the freezer. I love bread in all its forms, and if you haven't tried making salad of day-old bread, I think it's definitely time you tried panzanella.*

Tjälknöl

Preheat the convection oven to 160 °F (70 °C).
Place the frozen meat in an ovenproof dish. Cook in the oven for approximately 8 hours.
Bring the marinade ingredients to the boil then leave to cool. Place the baked meat in a bowl and pour over the brine. You can also put the meat in a vacuum bag or resealable plastic bag. Leave the meat to marinate in the refrigerator for at least 10 hours. Wipe off the meat with paper towels, cut into thin slices, and serve.

Pickled red onion

Peel and shred the onion. Measure out the other ingredients into a saucepan and bring to a rolling boil. Place the onions in a bowl and pour over the warm brine. Allow to cool and store in the refrigerator.

Panzanella

Dice the bread or tear it into large pieces and place in a large bowl. Rinse and quarter the tomatoes and cucumber and add to the bread. Add vinegar, olive oil, salt, and pepper. Add the remaining ingredients and stir. Season and serve with the meat.

Preparation
10 minutes
Cooking
5–10 minutes
Makes
2 portions

approx. 7 oz. (200 g)
sliced *tjälknöl* (see page 57)
4 slices white bread
3½ oz. (100 g) sliced Comté or
other quality mature cheese
butter
waffle iron

Tjälknöl croque monsieur

It's said that the first croque monsieur was served in Paris in the 1910s. Back then, it was probably a couple of slices of ham that accompanied the mature cheese in this classic hot double sandwich. Here we've made it with slow-cooked moose steak. The only difficult thing about this recipe is remembering to bring the waffle iron. Otherwise, it's a simple, tasty recipe for a day out or a hunting lunch.

Butter the slices of bread. Arrange the cheese and *tjälknöl* on two of the slices of bread. Arrange into double sandwiches and pack in plastic wrap or greaseproof paper. Remember to take the waffle iron and extra butter with you.

Heat the waffle iron in the fire, add the butter, and allow it to melt. Grill the sandwiches until the bread is a beautiful golden brown.

Preparation
40 minutes
Cooking
30 minutes
Makes
4 portions

Moose steak
1¼–1¾ lb. (600–800 g)
   moose steak
oil and butter
salt and black pepper

Fried green asparagus
1 bunch green asparagus
lemon juice
butter
salt and black pepper

Green peppercorn sauce
1 tbsp. black peppercorns
2 tbsp. pickled green
   peppercorns, chopped
1 shallot
1 tbsp. butter
2 tbsp. cognac
1¼ cups (300 ml) game stock
   (see page 80)
1¼ cups (300 ml) whipping
   cream
1 tsp. liquid from the pickled
   green peppercorn jar
sherry vinegar
lemon juice
cornstarch, as needed
salt

To serve
fresh French fries

Moose steak with green peppercorn sauce

It's often the sauce that determines whether a dish is merely good or outstanding. So spend time on getting the sauce right and the moose and its accompaniments will really come into their own. The sauce contains green as well as black peppercorns, the latter of which have a little more bite. To make the black peppercorns a little milder, I blanch them rapidly twice so their flavor isn't so dominant.

Moose steak

Preheat the convection oven to 300 °F (150 °C).
Remove any sinews from the meat. Divide the beef into
   4 portions.
Fry the meat until nicely golden brown in equal parts butter
   and oil in a frying pan over a high heat. Season with salt
   and pepper. Place the meat in an ovenproof dish and bake
   in the center of the oven until the internal temperature
   is 118 °F (48 °C)—this will be 133 °F (56 °C) final temperature.
   Remove the meat from the oven and leave to rest for at least
   5 minutes before serving.

Green peppercorn sauce

Blanch the black peppercorns quickly twice: Bring the water to the boil in two small saucepans. Add the black peppercorns to one saucepan. Leave the peppercorns to boil for a few seconds, then strain off the water and immediately place the peppercorns in the other saucepan. Strain again and lay the peppercorns on paper towels to cool. Allow to dry completely and then coarsely blend in a coffee mill, or place the peppercorns in a tea towel on a cutting board and crush using the handle of a large knife or mallet.

Coarsely chop the green peppercorns. Peel and finely chop the shallot. Fry the shallot in butter in a saucepan over a high heat until it begins to brown. Add the green and black peppercorn, cognac, and stock. Bring to the boil, then lower to medium heat. Add the cream and allow to simmer for approximately 15 minutes. Add the liquid from the green peppercorn jar and a splash each of sherry vinegar and lemon juice, and season. If necessary, thicken the sauce with cornstarch.

Fried green asparagus

Rinse and trim the asparagus. Heat the butter in a frying pan over a high heat. Fry the asparagus for about 2 minutes and finish with a splash of lemon juice, salt, and a few turns with the pepper mill.

Serve the moose with the green peppercorn sauce, asparagus, and crispy French fries.

Moose

Preparation
40 minutes
Cooking
2 hours
Makes
4 portions

Moose roulades
8 × 3 ½-oz. (100-g) slices
  of moose bottom round
1 carrot
5 ½ oz. (150 g) smoked
  pork belly
1 pickled gherkin
½ onion
4 tbsp. Dijon mustard
4 tbsp. curly parsley,
  coarsely chopped (save
  a little for the garnish)
¾ cup + 4 tsp. (200 ml) water
1 ¼ cups (300 ml) game stock
  (see page 80)
rapeseed oil and butter
salt and black pepper
twine or toothpicks

Cream sauce
¾ cup + 4 tsp. (200 ml)
  liquid from braising
  the roulades
1 ¼ cups (300 ml) whipping
  cream
4 tbsp. prunes
sherry vinegar
salt

To serve
flat-leaf parsley
boiled or mashed potatoes
  (see page 137)
pickled gherkin
blackcurrant jelly

Moose roulades in cream sauce

*Roulades are a true classic, and when you bite into this com-
bination of moose meat, salty gherkin, Dijon mustard, and
pork belly, it's easy to picture yourself in a stylish restaurant
from an earlier time. These moose roulades taste great
all by themselves, but the sauce takes them to another level.*

Moose roulades

Peel the carrots and cut into strips (the same length as the
  meat slices are wide). Cut the smoked pork belly and pickled
  gherkin into strips. Peel and coarsely slice the onion.
Place the meat slices on a work surface covered in plastic
  film, or a large cutting board. Salt and pepper, then brush
  the top with mustard. Sprinkle with chopped parsley, and
  lay a strip each of carrot, smoked pork belly, and pickled
  gherkin, as well as a few strips of onion, in the center of
  the meat. Roll up the roulades, and either tie them with
  twine or insert a couple of toothpicks so they stay together
  when cooked.
Fry the roulades until golden brown in equal parts butter and
  oil in a cast-iron frying pan. Season with salt and pepper
  while they cook. Add water and stock and bring to a rolling
  boil. Reduce to a low heat and cover the pan with the lid
  ajar. Leave the roulades to simmer for about 1 ½ hours,
  turning from time to time and adding a little more liquid
  if necessary.

Check whether they're done with a fork. The meat should be completely tender, and you should almost be able to twirl the fork. Remove the roulades and sieve the liquid for use in the sauce. Leave the roulades to cool a little and remove the twine/toothpicks. Make the sauce, then place the roulades in it and serve.

Cream sauce

Pour ¾ cup plus 4 tsp. (200 ml) of the cooking liquid into a saucepan and bring to the boil. Add the cream and prunes. Reduce to medium heat and allow to cook for approximately 10 minutes. Blend the sauce and season with a splash of sherry vinegar and a little salt. Place the roulades in the sauce and put the pan back over a low heat. Allow the roulades to simmer for a few minutes so they are properly hot again before serving.

To serve

Top the roulades with a little coarsely chopped parsley and serve with boiled or mashed potatoes, pickled gherkins, and blackcurrant jelly.

Memories of Hunting

It's unreal. Like a film.

It's a November day; an unusually warm one. There's a little rain in the air, but the visibility is good. I'm sitting at a spot on what's called Nya vägen—the New Road. The dogs have been close to my stand several times, so I'm right in the hunt, in the moment. Somewhere inside me, I feel that today might be the day I shoot my first moose. Suddenly, a little way into the forest, I see a moose run past with a dog chasing it. The moose doesn't come out far enough, but my pulse goes up anyway. I take a few deep breaths and try to focus on my surroundings again. Just a few minutes later, there's another noise.

A bull moose comes out 50 yards to my left and stands by the road. There's no dog chasing after it. It steps calmly out and stops with a perfect broadside toward me. I take aim. My pulse thuds in my temples. I run through the checklist in my head. Is it legal game? It is a sure shot? I'm thinking, yet not thinking. Instinct takes over, and I fire.

—Micke

Preparation
20 minutes
Cooking
20 minutes
Makes
4 portions

1 ¾ lb. (800 g) mixed
   game meat, diced
1 ¼ lb. (600 g) waxy
   potatoes, washed
1 onion
2 cups (400 ml)
   chanterelles
1 ½ cups (300 ml)
   whipping cream
4 eggs
4 tbsp. fresh or frozen
   lingonberries
2 tbsp. curly parsley,
   coarsely chopped
rapeseed oil and butter
salt and black pepper

Hunter's hash

Unfortunately, when you butcher and trim meat, there are often leftovers that either get turned into ground meat or, worse, don't get used at all. But here's a tip. Dice the trimmings immediately, put in a freezer bag, label "hash meat," and freeze. When you have enough of these bags in your freezer, you can get them out and make a delicious game hash on the griddle for your hunter friends or your family to enjoy.

Leave the frozen meat to thaw in the refrigerator overnight. Dice the potatoes into ½-in. (1-cm) cubes. Peel and finely chop the shallot. Trim the mushrooms.

Set the griddle over a high heat and add enough of equal parts oil and butter. Fry the potatoes for 5 minutes, stirring constantly, then season with salt and pepper. Add the meat and onion and allow to fry for a further 5 minutes. Check the seasoning. Add the mushrooms and cream and reduce to a low heat. Allow to simmer gently for a couple of minutes.

Fry the egg on the other side of the pan with a little oil and butter, and season again if necessary. Top the hash with lingonberries and parsley.

69

WILD BOAR

It's time for blind hunting for wild boar, which are causing havoc with the crops.

Since wild boar appeared in Sweden in earnest about 50 years ago, boar hunting has increased continuously. At the same time, culling has increased enormously since the 1990s. Locally, wild boar can cause significant damage to plantations and seeds if they get the taste for things like wheat, oats, potatoes, or freshly sown clover. And in addition to eating, they root around and trample the fields. Feeding wild boar in the forest using a timer-controlled feeder means you can keep them far away from cultivated fields. Hunting them at these feeding points isn't as dramatic as other forms of hunting, but the major advantage is that you have plenty of time to choose which animal to shoot, and it will usually be standing still as you fire. We can almost guarantee that the wild boar will come by the feeding point every night. Then it's all about whether the hunter happens to be sitting in the right place when they appear.

It's much more dramatic to hunt wild boar by driving them, as 10–15 animals can come running through the stand at once, and you have to think quickly to deal with them. Always shoot the smallest animal in the herd, although not the striped ones that weigh only a few pounds and give almost no meat. Sows with piglets are always protected because the current year's piglets won't survive on their own. Boar live in a matriarchal group,

so shooting the alpha female would also create major problems in the group. If you shoot a younger boar in the herd near a meadow where the animals are causing damage, it seems that the alpha female understands to keep away from there, at least for a few weeks. The males tend to be solitary and seek out the herd when the sow comes into heat. In general, the meat of a male develops a particular flavor, known as boar taint, when the sow is in heat, which isn't optimal for cooking. A good way to find out whether the meat has boar taint is to cut off a bit of the meat and burn it with a soldering iron. You can tell from the smell whether it's tainted. If it turns out that the meat does have boar taint, I suggest you make spicy sausages with it, using a lot of garlic and chili. If you shoot boar weighing only up to about 130 lb. (60 kg), there's no risk of encountering boar taint.

One thing I think you should bear in mind is not to get stressed about firing at the boar a second time. If you're sitting in a tower with good support and animals are appearing at a moderate pace and perhaps stopping and giving you a good firing position at a distance of 165–230 ft. (50–70 m), you should be able to feel certain that the first shot will strike where it should—instead of being nervous and immediately firing a second shot just because the animal continues moving forward. With experience,

Blood on the ground indicates a clean shot. A clean shot needn't mean the boar is lying dead right there. A boar that's been shot can run approximately 65 ft. (50 m). On this occasion, when we found the animal, we noted a perfect strike right behind the shoulders.

you learn that the second shot is always a bad one. If your strike hits the shoulders, it isn't always the case that the animal drops on the spot and dies immediately. It may run on for 80–100 ft. (25–30 m) first. There's no reason to panic. Since the boar will run after the first shot, you have to aim a little ahead of the animal when you take a second shot; there's a risk of hitting the rumen (stomach) and having the bullet go out through it and into the rear leg. Then you've unnecessarily destroyed a big section of the usable parts of the animal, and that's not good hunting.

Boar hunting is safe as long as you aren't careless, but if you don't hit where you intended it can be dangerous. If you're sitting waiting during a drive hunt and decide to fire at a male, and your shot's a bad one that hits it in the stomach, it's important that you don't start searching for it without a dog. It's not unlikely that the injured boar will try to attack you if you start following it. Instead, wait for a dog and allow it to bay the animal so you have the chance to shoot safely.

Wild boar

Wild boar are the ancestors of our domestic pigs, but extensive hunting and hybridization with domestic pigs meant they were all but gone from most Swedish forests by the early 1700s. It wasn't until the 1970s that they began to return, when escaped animals from wild boar enclosures began to establish populations in Sweden. Today, wild boar can be found over large parts of southern Sweden, and it's likely this geographical expansion will continue.

Biology & ecology

Male: boar
Female: sow
Young: piglet

Fully grown sows can weigh upward of 220 lb. (100 kg), boars twice that. The piglets are striped during the first few months of life, after which the coat becomes a uniform dark color in winter and a little lighter in the summer. The coat changes twice per year. The males' canines in the lower jaw are larger than those of the females. Wild boar are omnivores and primarily live on roots, nuts, acorns, leaves, and fallen fruit, but also eat insects, worms, and small rodents. After the rut, which involves considerable fighting between the boars, the sows give birth to 3–6 piglets. Older sows often produce more young. The piglets gain weight quickly. After just 6 months, they weigh around 65 lb. (30 kg).

Hunting periods

Wild boar (except for sows with striped or small brown piglets): entire Sweden April 1–January 31.
Wild boar, yearlings: entire Sweden July 1–June 30.
Local variations occur. Check with the County Administrative Board where you're going to hunt. Wild boar may be hunted at any time of day or night.

Types of hunting

Stalking, blind hunting, and hunting with dogs are the most common hunting methods.

Dogs

Dogs used to close contact with game and which are mentally strong, such as hunting spitzes or terriers.

Weapons

Class 1 rifles. Single bore shotguns of caliber 12, 16, or 20 may be used with lead shot.

Designated targets

Primarily piglets (not the very smallest ones) and yearlings. Sows with piglets may not be shot.

Preparation
10 minutes
Cooking
5 hours
Makes
enough for a good
number of containers
to keep in the freezer

2 ¼ lb. (1 kg) pork ribs
approx. 4 ½ lb. (2 kg) wild boar
    bones, moose bones, or
    other game bones, sawn
2 onions
3–4 sprigs thyme
4–5 qt. (4–5 liters) water

Game stock

This stock is best if you use completely fresh bones, but it works well with bones frozen immediately after being butchered, too. When I make game stock, I often add a little farm-reared pork to make the stock extra rich and tasty. I generally use only onions as the vegetable when I'm making stock. You can add other vegetables, but I think the sweetness of the root vegetables tends to take over—and it's the richness of the meat flavor that I'm after.

Preheat the convection oven to 440 °F (225 °C).
Divide the ribs along the bone and mix with the game bones
    in an ovenproof dish. Roast in the center of the oven for
    approximately 15 minutes, then turn the bones and roast
    for another 15 minutes.
Cut the onions in half and place in a frying pan with the cut
    face downward. Fry over a high heat for approximately
    2 minutes. Don't remove the onions until the cut face is
    almost black.
Transfer the bones, but not the fat, to a saucepan. Add the
    thyme and onion and cover with cold water. Place the
    saucepan over a high heat and allow to come to the boil.
    Skim the stock, then lower the heat. Leave the stock
    to simmer gently for approximately 4 hours, topping up
    with a little water if the bones aren't fully covered.
Sieve the onion and bones from the stock and replace over a
    high heat. Allow the stock to come to the boil, sieve again,
    and reduce to medium heat. Allow the stock to reduce to
    approximately half the volume. Sieve again. It's a good idea
    to pour the stock into smaller containers and freeze it,
    so you can just thaw the quantity you need.

Preparation
approx. 6 hours,
including brining
Cooking
5–6 minutes for
sausage and stock
Makes
4 portions +
extra sausages

Stock
2 ¼ cup (600 ml) game stock
  (see page 80)
2 bay leaves
1 tsp. salt
Tabasco, chili flakes,
  or chili oil (optional)

Homemade sausage
4 ½ lb. (2 kg) wild boar, minced
½ cup sauerkraut, chopped
4 tbsp. roast onion
2 ½ tbsp. salt
1 tsp. black pepper
2 cups crushed ice or
  iced water
sheep sausage casings,
  soaked
sausage stuffer or piping bag
  for filling the casings

Wild boar sausages in stock

Instead of coffee, a vacuum flask of hot stock with a little spice is my favorite thing when I'm waiting at a stand on a chilly fall or winter's day. And if you'd like to make this pick-me-up a bit more filling, here's a recipe for wild game sausage. Of course, you can also add store-bought sausages to the stock, because making sausages is a little onerous, but as with other time-consuming food, when you taste the result, you'll probably think it's time well spent.

Homemade sausage

Mix the ground meat, sauerkraut, salt, and pepper in a chilled
    bowl. Add the crushed ice/ice water and stir so that it's all
    well mixed and the filling binds together.
With the casings in a water-filled ovenproof dish or other
    container, fill them with the sausage mixture. Make sure
    you avoid air pockets. Twist the filled casings to make
    the sausages of the required size, or tie with twine. Place
    a damp tea towel over the sausages and set them aside in
    the refrigerator overnight to brine (or for at least 6 hours).

Stock

Bring all the stock ingredients to the boil in a saucepan.
    Season with salt and spice (Tabasco, chili flakes, or chili oil).
Prick the sausages with a skewer and cook in the stock
    by carefully simmering them to an internal temperature
    of 160 °F (70 °C). This should take about 5 minutes.

Preparation
40 minutes + brining the
sausages, at least 6 hours
Cooking
30 minutes
Makes
4 portions +
extra sausages

Sausage
3¼ lb. (1.5 kg) wild boar meat,
 ground
5½ oz. (160 g) pork fat
4 garlic cloves
1 tbsp. chili flakes
3½ tbsp. ground paprika
¾ cup + 4 tsp. (200 ml)
 red wine
2½ tbsp. salt
1¼ cups (300 ml) crushed ice
pig sausage casings
rapeseed oil and butter

Mashed potato
10 oz. (275 g) starchy
 potatoes, peeled
3½ tbsp. butter
⅓ cup (75 ml) milk
salt

Cucumber salad
½ cucumber
1 scallion
½ red chili
¼ lemon
1 tbsp. basil, chopped
olive oil
salt and black pepper

To serve
4 flatbreads
roast onion
sriracha hot chili sauce

Wild boar salsiccia in flatbreads

*Filled flatbreads may often fall into the "fast food" category,
but if you make your own sausages, it's very slow fast food!
In Sweden, it's said that flatbreads were invented at a fast-
food joint in Stockholm in the 1960s. I say that's a wonderful
story! But whatever the truth, flatbread fillings can be varied
endlessly. Here's a recipe for a spicy wild boar sausage.*

Sausage

Place a large bowl, or the bowl from your food processor, in
 the refrigerator to chill. Dice the pork fat and place in the
 refrigerator. Place the sausage casing in cold water and
 flush through with water. Peel and finely chop the garlic,
 and mix with the chili flakes, ground paprika, and wine.
Remove the bowl from the refrigerator and mix all the ingredients except the ice with a wooden spoon, or a mixing
 blade if you're using a food processor. Work it into a well-
 blended mixture, add the crushed ice and blend again.
Put the mixture in a piping bag, or attach a sausage stuffer
 attachment to the food processor, and fill the sausage
 casings. Make sure the mixture is evenly spread along
 the casing. Knot or tie into uniform-sized sausages.
 Place the sausages in a lightly moistened tray, cover
 with plastic film, and set in the refrigerator overnight
 (or for at least 6 hours).
To serve, fry as many sausages as you need in a pan with oil
 and butter, or grill until the sausages are cooked through
 and nicely browned.

Cucumber salad

Rinse and deseed the cucumber. Cut into ½-in. (1-cm) cubes and place in a bowl. Trim and finely shred the scallions. Rinse and finely chop the chili. Wash the lemon and grate the peel.

Mix everything in a bowl, season with a little olive oil, salt, and a few turns of the pepper mill. Mix well and serve with the sausage. If you make the cucumber salad in advance, you can store it in the refrigerator. However, it will produce a little liquid, so you'll need to sieve it before serving.

Mashed potato

Carefully peel and cook the potatoes. Drain the potatoes when they are cooked and allow the steam to dissipate. Mash the potatoes and add half of the butter. Warm the milk and add to the potatoes, a little at a time. Stir with a whisk or large spoon. Add the remaining butter and stir again. Season with salt and a few turns of freshly ground pepper to taste.

To serve

Arrange mashed potato, sausage, cucumber salad, roast onion, and sriracha on each flatbread and roll up.

**Wild boar salsiccia
in flatbreads**

Preparation
approx. 40 minutes.
For the best flavor, you
can make the piccalilli
a couple of days before.
Cooking
5 minutes
Makes
6 portions

Wild boar Scotch eggs
14 oz. (400 g) wild boar,
  minced
6 + 1 eggs
1½ tsp. salt
1 tsp. dried sage
1 tsp. dried tarragon
1 tsp. dried oregano
1 pinch cayenne pepper
rapeseed oil/frying oil
  for deep frying
salt

For the breading
4¼ oz. (120 g) wheat flour
2 eggs
¾ cup + 4 tsp. (200 ml)
  panko breadcrumbs

Piccalilli
3½ oz. (100 g) zucchini
3½ oz. (100 g) cauliflower
3½ oz. (100 g) carrots
3½ oz. (100 g) onion
3½ oz. (100 g) celery root
2 tsp. salt
2 tsp. turmeric
2 tsp. coriander seeds
2 tsp. yellow mustard seeds
1 cup + 2 tsp. (250 ml)
  white wine vinegar
6 tbsp. (90 g) sugar
1 tbsp. cornstarch

Wild boar Scotch eggs

This egg dish is great either hot or cold, and it makes a perfect satisfying picnic at a stand in the forest when the hunt's running over or for the hunt lunch. The ground meat stays together a little better if you grind it twice. Piccalilli, or mustard pickle, is a British condiment containing pickled vegetables that works perfectly with a Scotch egg, and with many other foods, too. Make a big batch while you're at it!

Piccalilli

Trim and chop the vegetables and remove the seeds from the zucchini. All the vegetables should be roughly the same, bite size, so that they cook in around the same time. Place the vegetables in a bowl and add the salt and other spices. Stir thoroughly, cover the bowl with plastic film, and leave to stand at room temperature for approximately 2 hours.

Drain off the liquid released by the vegetables. Put the vinegar, sugar, and cornstarch in a saucepan and bring to the boil, stirring constantly. Add the vegetables and simmer gently over a low heat for about 3–4 minutes. Pour the vegetables into a glass jar or other suitable container. Leave to cool and store in a cool, dark place.

Once opened, store in the refrigerator. The piccalilli tastes best if it's allowed to stand for a couple of days before serving. Serve with Scotch eggs, though it also works well with cooked meat, fried fish, or in a sandwich.

Wild boar Scotch eggs

Carefully place 6 eggs in a saucepan of boiling water and boil for 5–6 minutes (the yolk should be creamy), then run them under cold water.

Mix the ground meat, salt, spices, and 1 egg in a bowl. Form into 6 equal balls.

Shell the boiled eggs. Flatten one of the balls of ground meat between damp hands, then fold the meat mixture around the egg. Repeat with the remaining eggs.

Prepare separate bowls with the flour, lightly beaten egg, and panko breadcrumbs. Bread the eggs in the same order—first the flour, then the beaten egg, and finally the breadcrumbs.

Deep-fry in oil at 350 °F (175 °C) until golden brown on every side. Lift the eggs onto a plate covered with paper towel. Salt and allow to cool a little before packing them to take into the forest.

If you don't want to deep-fry your Scotch eggs, you can place them in a lightly greased ovenproof dish and bake in an oven for 4–5 minutes at 440 °F (225 C°) until they are nicely browned.

Preparation
30 minutes
Cooking
1½ hours
Makes
4 portions

Tomato sauce
½ carrot
¼ celery stalk
1 banana shallot
2 garlic cloves
3½ oz. (100 g) pancetta
7 tbsp. (100 ml) red wine
¾ cup + 4 tsp. (200 ml)
   game stock (see page 80)
1 tbsp. dried oregano
1¾ lb. (800 g) canned whole
   peeled tomatoes
olive and rapeseed oil
salt and black pepper

Meatballs
1¼ lb. (600 g) wild boar,
   minced
4 tbsp. breadcrumbs
3½ tbsp. (50 ml) dry
   white wine
2 eggs
½ garlic clove
10 tbsp. Parmesan, grated
2 tsp. dried oregano
2 tsp. salt
black pepper

To serve
freshly cooked pasta
grated Parmesan
shredded basil
grated lemon zest
olive oil
black pepper

Wild boar meatballs in tomato sauce

This is a dish I often make at home. It's a version of Sunday sauce, and for me it's exactly what the name implies—a cozy Sunday afternoon in the kitchen with tomato sauce simmering gently at the back of the hob. It's best cooked for a long time, but remember to dilute it with more stock or water now and then. You can finish it by adding the meatballs at roughly the time you put the pasta water on to boil.

Tomato sauce

Peel the carrots and chop into small cubes, approximately ⅒ in. (3 mm). Peel the celery and cut into cubes the same size. Peel and finely chop the onion and garlic. Finely dice the pancetta.

Fry the carrot, celery, shallot, garlic, and pancetta in equal parts rapeseed and olive oil in a deep-sided saucepan or cast-iron casserole dish for approximately 4–5 minutes on a medium heat, stirring continuously.

Pour over the wine and bring to the boil. Then add the game stock, oregano, and tomatoes, and bring to the boil again before reducing the heat to low. Simmer for approximately one hour with the lid ajar, diluting with more water if necessary.

Meatballs

Soak the breadcrumbs in the wine in a medium bowl. Stir and add the egg, then stir again and add the ground meat. Mix well and season with grated garlic, Parmesan, oregano, salt, and pepper. Combine everything thoroughly with a wooden spoon, or a mixing blade if you're using a food processor.

Form into meatballs in your palm using a spoon. Dip the spoon into a glass of warm water from time to time, to help the meatballs more easily.

Place the meatballs in the casserole dish and allow to simmer in the sauce for at least 20 minutes. Serve with freshly cooked pasta, and ideally Parmesan, basil, lemon zest, olive oil, and more pepper.

Memories of Hunting

A dog is a hunter's best friend, but sometimes accidents happen. I was once taking part in a hunt on a large estate in Sweden with Lisa, my German Shorthaired Pointer. It was a wild boar hunt, and many piglets in the 25–30-kg (55–65-lb.) class had been shot. The last remaining quarry was a huge sow weighing more than 150 kg (330 lb.). Lisa got more and more excited the longer the hunt went on, and amid all the commotion the sow managed to get hold of Lisa's back end. I didn't see it myself, but another dog handler called on the radio to say my dog was bleeding slightly from one of its hind legs.

Lisa was so hyped on adrenaline that when she came to me, she just seemed to be limping a little. When I felt her leg, I could tell immediately that something was seriously wrong. I set off with her to the vet straightaway, and once there it turned out that two major muscle groups had been completely severed. Lisa was immediately taken into the operating room. After a whole year's convalescence, Lisa was back in the forest, but from that moment on she never barked at a boar again, not even if she ended up among a whole pack of them.

—Hubbe

Preparation
45 minutes + 3–4 hours
pasta dough resting time
Cooking
10 minutes
Makes
4 portions

Pasta dough
2 cups (280 g) semolina flour
2 eggs
3 egg yolks
2 tbsp. olive oil

Filling
11 oz. (300 g) wild boar,
 ground
1 egg
½ garlic glove
10 tbsp. grated Parmesan
1 ¾ oz. (50 g) ricotta
1 tsp. salt
2 tsp. sage, chopped
black pepper

Deep-fried garlic
2 heads of solo garlic
¾ cup + 4 tsp. (200 ml) milk
oil for deep frying

To serve
1 cup + 2 tbsp. (250 g) butter
fresh sage leaves
Parmesan
black pepper

Wild boar ravioli

This is a very simple dish, but one that involves a lot of effort—and love. In other words, the same ingredients as many of the best dishes.

To make good pasta you should listen to your instincts. If the dough feels dry and stiff, add a few drops of cold water. If it feels too sticky, add a little more flour.

Pasta dough

If you don't want to make the pasta dough in the food processor, you can do it directly on the worktop or in a bowl. Weigh out the flour and pour it into the food processor. Beat the egg and olive oil in a bowl. Begin blending the flour in the food processor, and add the egg mixture. Blend for approximately 30 seconds, until it forms small crumbs about the same size as couscous. Pour out onto the work surface and knead into a dough. Wrap the dough in plastic and leave to stand in the refrigerator for at least 4 hours. Remove the dough at least an hour before making the ravioli so it has time to reach room temperature.

Filling

Weigh the filling and place in a bowl, add the remaining ingredients and mix well. Transfer the filling to a piping bag or shape into small balls and place on a baking tray. Store in the refrigerator until you have rolled out the pasta dough.

Ravioli

If you don't have a pasta machine, you'll have to use a tradition-al rolling pin. Lightly flour the room-temperature dough, then roll out a strip approximately 6 in. (15 cm) wide to the minimum thinness on the pasta machine, or as thin as you can with the rolling pin. Divide the strip lengthways. Pipe out small portions of filling on one strip, or place out the premade meatballs. If necessary, brush with a little water or egg yolk. Cover with the remaining pasta strip. Press around the filling so that the pasta stays together and any air is expelled. Cut out the ravioli with a pasta cutter or a regular knife and place on greased paper or a lightly floured baking sheet. Ravioli also freeze very well, and then can be cooked directly from frozen.

Deep-fried garlic

Peel and thinly slice the garlic with a mandoline or slice it as thinly as possible with a sharp knife. Leave the garlic slices to soak in milk in the refrigerator for at least 2 hours.
Sieve the garlic and leave to drain. Fry in batches in a deep fryer or saucepan. The oil should be at 355 °F (180 °C). Remove the garlic chips when they are golden brown. Leave to drain on paper towels, then salt.

To serve

Boil the pasta water. Cube the butter and melt it in a frying pan over a medium heat, stirring from time to time. When the butter has browned and developed a pleasant, nutty scent, remove the frying pan from the heat and add the sage leaves.
Place the ravioli in the pasta water and lower the heat until it's just simmering. Simmer for approximately 2 minutes (depending on the size of the pasta—taste it to be sure). Drain the ravioli and place into the sage butter. Stir and top with deep-fried garlic, grated Parmesan, and a few turns of black pepper.

Wild Boar

**Grilled wild boar
ham steak**

Preparation
40 minutes
Cooking
40 minutes
Makes
4 portions

Potato gratin
1¾ lb. (800 g) waxy potatoes
2 onions
1–2 garlic cloves
7 tbsp. (100 g) butter
1½ cups (400 ml) whipping
    cream
1 tbsp. juice of squeezed
    lemon
2 tsp. dried thyme
5¼ oz. (150 g) Gruyère, grated
salt

Flintastek
approx. 1¾ lb. (800 g)
    wild boar ham steak, sliced
rapeseed oil
salt and black pepper

Herb & lemon oil
½ lemon
7 tbsp. herbs (e. g. parsley,
    thyme, chervil), chopped
1 garlic clove, grated
7 tbsp. (100 ml) olive oil
salt and black pepper

Tomato salad
9 oz. (250 g) red cherry
    tomatoes
9 oz. (250 g) yellow cherry
    tomatoes
1 red onion
2 tbsp. herb and lemon oil

Grilled wild boar ham steak

Flintastek *is a marinated ham steak that first became popular in Sweden in the 1960s, but really took off in the 1980s when it was renamed after* The Flintstones *TV animated sitcom. These days, Swedes tend to associate the dish with cheap, pre-marinated meat badly cooked over a disposable grill. But if you make* flintastek *from wild boar and serve it with a fresh tomato salad, the flavor will reward your effort ten times over.*

Potato gratin

Preheat the convection oven to 390 °F (200 °C). Grease an ovenproof dish with half of the butter. Cut the potatoes into slices approximately ⅛ in. (5 mm) thick and rinse in cold water. Peel the onions and slice slightly more thinly than the potatoes. Grate the garlic into a saucepan and add the cream and the rest of the butter. Warm over a medium heat, then remove the saucepan from the heat when the butter has melted and add the lemon juice and thyme. Place alternate layers of potatoes and onions in the dish, with a little melted butter, cheese, and salt for each layer. Finish with a layer of potatoes and topped with plenty of grated cheese. Bake on the middle rack for approximately 40 minutes.

Flintastek

Light the grill and wait until the coals are ready. Rub a little oil into the ham steaks. Season with salt and pepper. Grill over the hottest coals for about 2 minutes per side. Depending on the thickness of the meat, it may need to lie on a lower, indirect heat or go in a regular oven at 285 °F (140 °C) for a little while to reach the right internal temperature. I think 136–140 °F (58–60 °C) is a good final temperature, which means you can cook it to approximately 120–125 °F (50–52 °C) and then leave it to rest for about 5 minutes before serving.

Herb and lemon oil

Wash the lemon and grate the zest into a bowl. Add the lemon juice, herbs, salt, and pepper. Add the garlic and olive oil and mix well. Dress the tomato salad with the oil and top the meat with a little oil, too.

Tomato salad

Rinse the tomatoes. Peel and finely chop the red onion. Cut up the tomatoes and mix the onion and tomatoes with the herb and lemon oil.

Swedish vegetable soup
with grilled wild boar belly

Preparation
6 hours' brining
Cooking
4–5 hours' smoking
Makes
8 portions

Hot-smoked wild boar belly
approx. 4 ½ lb. (2 kg)
  boneless wild boar belly
grill or smoker
charcoal, briquettes,
  and small pieces or
  shavings of, for example,
  applewood

Brine
5 qt. (5 liters) water
3 tbsp. (50 g) iodine-free salt

Hot-smoked wild boar belly

Most things you can do with domestic pork can be done with wild boar—and bacon is always popular. This hot-smoked wild boar belly is an ingredient in several of my recipes, because it's a real favorite! Here I describe how to make it in a kettle grill, but if you have a smoker, the process is a bit easier to control.

Brine

Measure the cold water and add the salt. Whisk until the salt dissolves. Place the wild boar belly in a dish and cover with the brine. Place in the refrigerator and allow to brine for at least 6 hours.

Smoking

If you don't have access to a dedicated smoker, you can smoke the wild boar belly in a kettle grill. Light the grill using half of the charcoal and briquettes. Take advantage of the glowing coals by cooking something else in the meantime. Remove the wild boar belly from the brine and wipe off with paper towel. Wait until the temperature under the lid of the grill approaches 300 °F (150 °C). Place the wood chips and belly in the grill. Smoke for 4–5 hours at approximately 175 °F (80 °C). Leave the belly to cool and store in the refrigerator.

Preparation
30 minutes + 10 hours
if you're smoking the
belly first
Cooking
20 minutes
Makes
4 portions

Grilled wild boar belly
approx. 14 oz. (400 g)
  hot-smoked wild boar
  belly (see opposite)

Swedish vegetable soup
1 onion
1 carrot
½ pointed white cabbage
1 scallion
7 tbsp. (100 g) fresh peas
2 tbsp. butter
2 tbsp. wheat flour
1¼ cups (300 ml) milk
¾ cup + 4 tsp. (200 ml)
  whipping cream
¾ cup + 4 tsp. (200 ml)
  game stock (see page 80)
2 tsp. salt
grated nutmeg

Swedish vegetable soup with grilled wild boar belly

Ängamat, a kind of Swedish vegetable soup, literally means "meadow food." It's a dish Swedes tend to remember being cooked by their grandmothers. I don't recall it from my own childhood, and if it had been served to me, I probably wouldn't have liked it because of all the vegetables. Now I can't imagine a better combination than ängamat *with grilled hot-smoked wild boar belly.*

Swedish vegetable soup

Peel and finely chop the onion. Peel the carrot and cut into approximately ⅓-in. (1-cm) cubes. Trim and cut the cabbage into small pieces, approximately ⅓ × ⅓ in. (2×2 cm). Trim and shred the scallions.

Warm the butter in a saucepan over a medium heat. Add the onion, carrot, and cabbage and fry for a few minutes, stirring continuously to prevent browning. Season with salt. Add the flour and stir in thoroughly with a wooden spoon. Add the milk, cream, and stock. Bring to the boil then lower the heat. Allow to simmer for approx. 5 minutes, stirring from time to time. Add the scallions and peas. Season with salt and a little finely grated nutmeg. Dilute with a little milk or water as needed.

Grilled wild boar belly

Light the grill and wait until the coals are ready. Cut the hot-smoked belly into slices approximately ⅓ in. (1 cm) thick. Grill for about 1 minute on each side. Serve with the vegetable soup.

**Whole grilled
wild boar**

Preparation
30 minutes
Cooking
10 hours
Makes
8–12 portions

Whole grilled wild boar
1 whole small wild boar,
   approx. 18–33 lb. (8–15 kg)
sea salt and black pepper
rotisserie
steel wire, as needed
large grill or hearth

Brine
10 qt. (10 liters) water
7 tbsp. (120 g) iodine-free salt

Glaze
14 tbsp. (200 g) butter
1 garlic clove, finely grated
2 tbsp. tomato paste
2 tsp. dried thyme
3 tbsp. pink peppercorns,
   crushed
7 tbsp. (100 ml) honey
1 tbsp. sherry vinegar

Whole grilled wild boar

In my world, this makes for the perfect grill party—a barbecue with friends on an early summer's evening and with the weather on your side. Plan for the cooking to take the whole day, because it takes a long time and requires you to keep a close watch on the fire. Move a cutting board outdoors and make a prep station beside the grill area if you don't already have an outdoor kitchen.

So what do I serve with the wild boar? Ideally, at least one salad, and I'll probably grill some vegetables, too. A tasty vinaigrette, a real Béarnaise sauce, or a flavored mayonnaise all work well, and perhaps I'll also boil the first new potatoes of the year.

To regulate the heat, a rotisserie that can be raised and lowered is useful. If you don't have access to a powered rotisserie, you'll just have to set aside 5–6 hours to manually rotate the meat. If there are a few of you, this will be much easier because you can take it in turns!

Brine

Bring 2 cups (500 ml) of the water to the boil in a kettle or saucepan. Pour into a large bowl or bucket. Add the salt and stir until dissolved. Add the remaining cold water. Stir again. Place the wild boar in a plastic tray or similar container and pour over the brine so the meat is completely covered. Leave to brine in the refrigerator for at least 4 hours.

Glaze

Brown the butter in a saucepan. Mix the butter with all the rest of the ingredients in a bowl. Remember that brown butter sets if it's allowed to go cold, so, although it's a good idea to make the glaze in advance and store it in the refrigerator, it needs time to warm up again before you can use it.

Whole grilled wild boar

Light the grill or fire where you'll be cooking the wild boar. Count on it taking about 5–6 hours to grill a whole wild boar of this size.

Remove the wild boar from the brine and wipe off with paper towel. Thread the wild boar onto the spit and, if necessary, tie up the legs with steel wire. This step will depend on the equipment you have for the grilling. It's important that the wild boar is constantly cooked over an even heat.

When I grill a whole boar, I generally remove the loin filets when they reach 130 °F (55 °C). However, to make sure the rest of the wild boar is well cooked, I don't tend to use a thermometer but simply feel the meat with a roasting fork or a knife. The meat should feel tender all the way through.

Start to brush on the glaze in the last half an hour. By this point the heat should be so low that the glaze doesn't burn. Remove the wild boar from the grill/hearth and leave to rest for about 15 minutes before you start removing the meat. Top with sea salt and pepper.

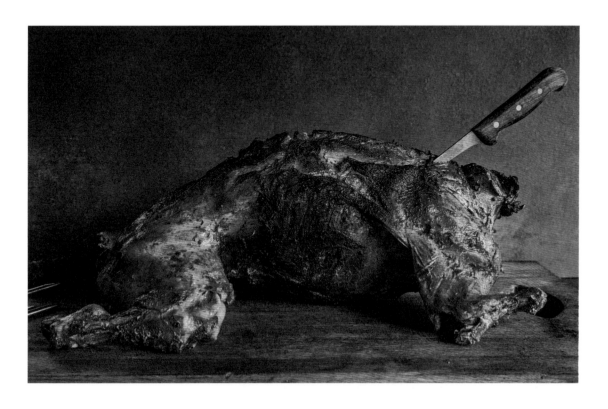

Preparation
30 minutes + 8 hours' brining
Cooking
2–3 hours
Makes
4 portions

Brined boiled wild boar leg
4 wild boar legs
5 qt. (5 liters) brine, 12%
1 onion
8–10 allspice berries
2 bay leaves

Parsley stock
1 shallot
1¼ cups (300 ml) liquid
   from cooking the legs
7 tbsp. (100 ml) whipping
   cream

1 bunch of curly parsley
2 tbsp. butter
rapeseed oil
salt

Accompaniments
1 kohlrabi
4 turnips
1 piece horseradish
2 tbsp. shredded flat-leaf
   parsley

Brined boiled wild boar leg

If you want to cook a traditional recipe and simply replace the customary brined pork leg with brined wild boar leg and serve it with mashed root vegetables, it will taste good. But here's a version with turnips, a wonderful foamy green sauce, and a kick of grated horseradish that I highly recommend.

Brined boiled wild boar leg

Place the legs in a saucepan and cover with brine. Brine in the refrigerator for at least 8 hours. Pour off the liquid and add new cold water to cover. Boil over a high heat and skim off the foam. Lower the heat to medium.

Peel and halve the onion and place in the saucepan together with the allspice and bay leaves. Allow to simmer for 2–3 hours, until the meat is completely tender (it should almost fall off the bone). Carefully remove from the liquid.

Parsley stock

Peel and finely chop the shallot and fry in a little rapeseed oil over a high heat. Add some liquid from cooking the legs, the milk, and the cream and bring to the boil. Reduce to a low heat and simmer for 10–15 minutes.

Trim and rinse the parsley. Pick off the leaves and place in a mixing bowl together with the butter. Pour the stock base over the parsley and blend on the highest speed for approximately 1 minute. Season with salt and serve the foamy stock with the leg.

Accompaniments & serving

Peel the kohlrabi and turnips and cut into wedges. Allow the vegetables to simmer with the legs over the last 5–10 minutes so they're just soft. Serve the meat and vegetables, pour over the stock, and top with grated horseradish and shredded parsley.

**Pulled wild
pork in pita**

Preparation
30 minutes + 1 hour's rising
time for the pita bread
Cooking
4–5 hours
Makes
4 portions

Pulled wild pork
1 ¾ lb. (800 g) wild boar
    shoulder, on the bone
2 tsp. salt
1 tbsp. soy sauce
7 tbsp. (100 ml) game stock
    (see page 80)
1 tsp. chili flakes
1 tbsp. ground paprika
1 tsp. dried thyme
1 tsp. caraway seed
2 garlic cloves

Pita bread (8 breads)
1 ½ lb. (750 g) wheat flour
    + 5 tbsp. (70 g)
    for kneading
2 cups (500 ml)
    lukewarm water
1 oz. (25 g) yeast
1 tsp. honey
1 tsp. salt
1 tbsp. olive oil

Harissa yogurt
7 tbsp. (100 ml) Turkish
    yogurt
7 tbsp. (100 ml) crème
    fraîche
2 tsp. harissa
salt and black pepper

Accompaniments
½ iceberg lettuce
2 tomatoes
1 bunch of cilantro
2 tbsp. pickled sliced
    jalapeños
2 scallions

Pulled wild pork in pita

Slow fast food is often the best food. A freshly baked pita, ideally cooked in a wood-fired oven, filled with pulled wild pork, salad, and sauce—it needn't be more complicated than that.

Pulled wild pork

Preheat the convection oven to 230 °F (110 °C).
Place the meat in a ceramic or cast-iron casserole dish with a lid. Rub the meat with spices and salt. Add the soy sauce, lightly crushed garlic cloves, and stock. Bake with the lid on in the center of the oven for approximately 4–5 hours. The meat should fall apart, and it should be very easy to remove the bones from the shoulder. Remove any hard sinews. Shred the meat using two forks, or allow it to cool slightly and do it with your hands. Serve the warm meat in the freshly baked pita breads.

Pita bread

Light the wood-fired oven (or set the oven to 480 °F / 250 °C after the initial rise). Place the yeast in a bowl and pour over the lukewarm water. Work it with a dough hook on your food processor or a wooden spoon if you're doing it by hand, until the yeast has dissolved. Add the other ingredients and work the dough until it's elastic, for approximately 5 minutes. Allow the dough to rise under a tea towel for 30 minutes. Make 8 equal-sized balls of dough on a lightly floured work surface and cover with a tea towel. Allow to rise for another 30 minutes at room temperature.

Powder the balls with a little flour and roll them out to approximately 6 in. (15 cm) in diameter. Bake in the wood-fired oven for about 2 minutes, rotating them carefully (without moving them, as the underside will burn) after half of the time. They should puff up and bake for a little while without developing any color. In a regular oven, you bake them on the middle rack of the oven on a baking tray with greaseproof paper for approximately 4 minutes (rotate carefully after approximately half of the time).

Harissa yogurt

Mix all the ingredients well in a bowl, and season with salt and pepper. Store in the refrigerator until serving.

Accompaniments & serving

Rinse and finely slice the lettuce. Rinse and dice the tomatoes. Coarsely chop the cilantro. Rinse and trim the scallions, then finely slice.

Fill the pita breads with a mixture of warm meat, lettuce, herbs, and jalapeño, and top with the harissa yogurt. Don't forget to provide paper napkins.

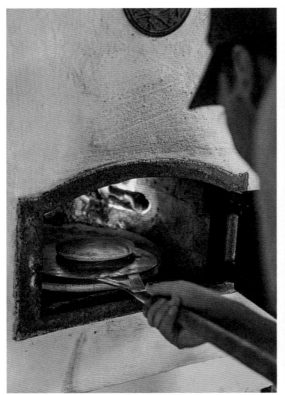

Wild Boar

ROE DEER

Before the roe deer hunting season begins on August 16, I take my full stock .222 out of the gun safe. I test-fire it, check the telescopic sight, and get out my tennis shoes, which allow me to move very quietly. At dawn or dusk, I tiptoe out. The feeling is amazing because it's the first real hunt of the season. Sometimes there's a low mist that lightens as the morning wears on, and I usually see lots of animals—bucks moving about and perhaps a doe and kid out in a meadow. But it's only the buck that needs to be on the alert for hunters. He'll often stand, stamping, in the bushes, not far from the doe. When he emerges, he's easily identified by his antlers, which can make a great trophy on your wall.

I always have one dog with me. If I take two dogs, things tend to get a bit rowdy. But you can go out alone, too. Where I go often depends on where I've seen roe deer earlier in the summer. If I've seen a buck at a particular forest edge near a meadow during the summer, I stealthily make my way there. Otherwise, you can simply sit by a meadow and wait. This isn't the time to fiddle with your cell phone. Sure enough, the roe deer appears, sometimes only 65 ft. (20 m) away. Stay constantly on the alert. As always when using a firearm, you need to make sure you have a good backstop for a safe shot. Often, there can be good opportunities for shots with this type of hunting. Perhaps the buck is grazing 260 ft. (80 m) away and you're sitting in a tower or have your rifle on a rest. At that distance, you should be able to hit an area the size of a coffee cup without difficulty. The buck will probably fall immediately after the shot, but sometimes it will still move away a little. Don't fire an unnecessary second shot if you know your first shot should have struck true. When you reach the place where the animal was standing, there are often clues. If you find hair, lung residues, and bright, foamy blood, these are indications that your shot struck home. You definitely don't want to find fragments of long bones, which indicate that you've struck a leg.

If you have access to a large hunting ground, you can be more mobile and move from one meadow to another, constantly keeping track of the wind direction. But it's in that moment right at dawn and dusk that the opportunities lie. And because you can't be in several places at once, you need to be lucky. During the day when it's warm, the buck stays in the forest, or rests up in the undergrowth.

Roe deer hunting using a Dachshund or other driving dog is also an enjoyable form of hunting. You release a Dachshund, which gets the scent of a roe deer, and because these dogs move quite slowly it's a calm drive and the roe deer moves slowly toward the stand shooter. If you hunt with larger, faster, flushing dogs, the roe deer often speed along as though fired from a cannon, and that makes it less easy to get a clear shot. If they're moving calmly, it can be a good idea to give a short, careful whistle. This makes them stop and look up, thus giving you a perfect shot. This works on the majority of large animals, but not wild boar— if you whistle at a boar, it will only move its legs even faster.

Later in the season, roe kids are legal game, but they're usually very small; sometimes too small to shoot, to my mind. But that's done in the same way as for buck hunting. In some places in Sweden, there's even spring buck hunting in May.

Roe deer

Roe deer hunting is popular, both because of the exciting hunt and the tasty meat. After being the game of royalty and the nobility for many years, in 1789 Swedish farmers were granted the right to hunt roe deer on their own land. This led to roe deer almost dying out in the 1800s. By the early 1900s, however, the population had recovered. Because roe deer eat newly planted trees, they can cause major damage.

Biology & ecology

Male: buck
Female: doe
Young: kid or fawn

A normal-sized roe deer weighs 45–65 lb. (20–30 kg), and significantly more in the late fall, when it's had a chance to fatten up, than in the spring. The population varies from one year to the next, depending in part on how mild or harsh the winter has been. Roe deer choose their food carefully. In the winter, they eat a lot of heather and brush and, if there's deep snow, even twigs; in the summer, this is supplemented with leaves and low-growing plants. Roe deer communicate with a sound that's like a short whistle, and if they hear a sudden noise, they can also give out a loud warning call.

Hunting periods

Roe deer: entire Sweden October 1–January 31.
Roe deer, antlered: entire Sweden August 16–September 30 and May 1–June 15 (only stalking or blind hunting).
Roe deer, kid: entire Sweden September 1–30 (only stalking or blind hunting). May be hunted from an hour before sunrise to an hour after sunset. During the hour after sunset, only stalking or blind hunting methods may be used. Local variations occur. Check with the County Administrative Board.

Types of hunting

Hunting with driving, short-distance driving and flushing dogs, or stalking. Blind hunting is a method that can be combined with stalking.

Dogs

Short-legged breeds such as the Dachshund and Drever as driving dogs, German Spaniels and Hunt Terriers for short-distance driving, and spaniels and retrievers as flushing dogs.

Weapons

Class 1 or 2 rifles and 20-caliber or larger shotguns.

Designated targets

There is no explicit target for roe deer management, but a general ethical rule not to shoot a doe with young.

Preparation
15 minutes
Cooking
6 hours
Makes
2–3 portions

Roe venison neck
approx. 2 lb. 14 oz. (1.3 kg)
 roe venison neck,
 on the bone
2 tsp. green juniper berries
2 tsp. salt
7 tbsp. (100 ml) white wine
7 tbsp. (100 ml) apple juice
7 tbsp. (100 ml) veal stock
black pepper
cornstarch or flour

Accompaniments
½ celery root
 (approx. 7 oz. / 200 g)
3 ½ oz. (100 g) smoked
 pork belly
1–2 apples
1 ½ tbsp. butter

Slow-cooked roe venison neck on the bone

A dish that works perfectly slow cooked overnight. Here the neck is cooked in a ceramic casserole, but of course it works just as well in any other ovenproof dish with a lid. Neck is one of my very favorite cuts, and it tastes especially good when you cook it on the bone. An alternative cut for this dish is bone-in shoulder. The meat should be completely tender and should easily come off the bone.

Roe venison neck

Preheat the convection oven to 390 °F (200 °C). Grind or coarsely chop the juniper berries and mixed with the salt. Rub the neck with the juniper salt, and, if possible, allow it to sit in the casserole for a couple of hours.

Next, place the casserole in the oven without the lid for approximately 15 minutes so that the meat browns slightly. Remove from the oven and add the wine, apple juice, and stock. Reduce the temperature to 210 °F (100 °C). Put the lid on the casserole and allow to simmer in the oven overnight (approximately 6 hours).

Remove the casserole and carefully lift out the neck. Leave the meat to cool on the cutting board. Divide up the meat. You should get two good bits from each side of the bone. You just follow the bone and make sure you get all the meat off. Cut away the sinews at the top.

Sieve the cooking liquid into a saucepan and place over a medium heat. Reduce until half the liquid remains, then season with salt and pepper. If necessary, thicken the sauce with cornstarch or flour. Place the meat in the sauce and allow to simmer until it's hot again.

Accompaniments

Peel the celeriac and cut into evenly sized pieces. Fry the pieces of celery root in butter in a frying pan over a medium heat. Meanwhile, cut the smoked pork belly into evenly sized strips and add to the pan. Core the apple and cut into wedges, then add them to the pan. Fry until the celeriac is soft but the apple wedges still have a little bite.

Preparation
1 hour
Cooking
1½ hours
Makes
4 portions

Roe venison steak
approx. 3 ½ lb. (1.6 kg)
  roe venison roast
  or other game roast
1 tsp. salt
oil, butter, and a
  few garlic cloves
black pepper
twine

***Hasselback* potatoes**
14 oz. (400 g) Amandine
  potatoes with skin
  or any waxy potatoes
7 tbsp. butter
3 tbsp. breadcrumbs
2 garlic cloves
salt

Café de Paris butter
1 cup + 3 tbsp.
  (250 g) butter
1 onion
½ garlic clove
1 tbsp. rapeseed oil
1 tsp. curry powder
1 tbsp. ketchup

1 tbsp. cognac
1 tsp. squeezed lemon juice
1 tsp. Dijon mustard
½ tsp. paprika
½ tsp. black pepper
½ tsp. cayenne pepper
½ tsp. dried tarragon
½ tsp. oregano
½ tsp. thyme
½ tsp. salt
1 tsp. elderberry capers
  or capers, chopped
1 tsp. anchovies, chopped

Green beans in vinaigrette
7 oz. (200 g) fresh green
  beans
1 onion
1 tbsp. Dijon mustard
1 tbsp. red wine vinegar
1 tsp. salt
1 tsp. sugar
2 tbsp. olive oil
2 tbsp. rapeseed oil
1 tbsp. fresh tarragon,
  chopped
freshly ground black pepper

Deboned whole roast leg of roe venison

This is a truly festive dish. If you've been lucky with your late-summer hunting, perhaps a fresh roe venison roast cooked in the outdoor kitchen will be the season's final meal on the patio. What could be nicer? That said, you can use this recipe all year round, and you can replace the roe venison roast with other game.

Roe venison steak

Preheat the convection oven to 350 °F (175 °C).
Remove the thighbone from the roast. Season with salt and
  pepper, then tie up the meat using the twine. If you want,
  you can also stuff the meat with herbs and lemon before you
  tie it up.
Fry the meat on all sides in oil and butter in a large frying pan
  over a high heat. Add a few whole garlic cloves. Place the
  browned roast in an ovenproof dish and set on the middle
  rack of the oven for approximately 20–30 minutes, until
  the internal temperature is 126 °F (52 °C).
Leave to rest for 10 minutes. Slice the meat and serve with
  the accompaniments.

Hasselback potatoes

Preheat the convection oven to 440 °F (225 °C) degrees. A trick when you're cutting *Hasselback* potatoes is to put the potato in a wooden spoon so you don't cut right through. Another trick is to even out the bottom of the potato so it sits more evenly on the cutting board. Make cuts at narrow intervals without cutting right through the potato. Rinse the potatoes in cold water and leave to dry on paper towel. Grease a baking tray or ovenproof dish with a little of the butter. Place potatoes in the tray—remember that they need to be quite close to each other to brown evenly.

Salt the potatoes and top with the rest of the butter. Add two whole garlic cloves to the tray. Bake the potatoes for 20-30 minutes, removing and basting the potatoes with butter from time to time. Sprinkle the breadcrumbs over the potatoes after half of the time, and continue baking until potatoes are done and have a nice golden-brown color.

Café de Paris butter

Dice the butter and place in a bowl. Allow the butter to come to room temperature (this takes approximately 1 hour).

Finely chop the onion and garlic and place in a saucepan with oil and the curry powder. Sweat over a medium heat for a couple of minutes. Remove from the heat and mix all the ingredients with the butter. Stir or whisk lightly so that everything mixes well.

Serve the butter as it is, or make rolls using greaseproof paper and place them in the refrigerator so you can cut slices off when serving.

Green beans in vinaigrette

Peel and finely chop the shallot. Place the onion in a bowl and add the Dijon mustard, vinegar, salt, and sugar. Whisk until the salt and sugar has dissolved. Add the rapeseed oil and olive oil a little at a time, continuing to whisk so that the vinaigrette emulsifies (thickens). Finish with the tarragon and a few turns of the black pepper mill.

Trim the beans and cook them in plenty of salted water for approximately 2 minutes. Drain the beans into a colander and place in the vinaigrette bowl, stirring so that the beans are well covered in vinaigrette.

Preparation
30 minutes
Cooking
30 minutes
Makes
4 portions

Loin of roe venison
1 lb. (500 g) loin of roe
  venison or other game
11 oz. (300 g) Jerusalem
  artichokes
3½ tbsp. butter
4 onions
3 tsp. sugar
7 oz. (200 g) Brussels
  sprouts
2 sprigs thyme
salt and black pepper
oil and butter
olive oil

Red wine sauce
1 onion
7 tbsp. (100 ml) red wine
2½ cups (600 ml)
  game stock (see page 80)
1 garlic clove
2 sprigs thyme
salt and black pepper
oil

Pink roast loin of roe venison

Roe deer are perhaps the most discerning of game animals when it comes to what they eat—they love to eat from herby meadows, and this is reflected in the flavor of the meat. Loin of roe venison is extremely tender and flavorful and can be paired with many different accompaniments. Here I serve it with roast Jerusalem artichokes, onions, and Brussels sprouts.

Loin of roe venison

Preheat the convection oven to 345 °F (175 °C). Rinse and brush the Jerusalem artichokes or scrape with a knife, halve them if they are large. Place them in an ovenproof dish with half of the butter and a little salt. Roast in the oven for approximately 15 minutes.

Trim and halve the onions, or cut into wedges if they are large. Remove the dish of Jerusalem artichokes from the oven and arrange the onion pieces in it. Continue to roast in the oven for about a further 15 minutes.

Trim and halve half of the Brussels sprouts. Remove the dish from the oven and arrange the halved Brussels sprouts in it. Roast for a further 5–10 minutes. Trim and remove the leaves from the remaining Brussels sprouts.

Meanwhile, trim any membrane from the loin and cut into four evenly sized pieces. Season the meat with salt and pepper on both sides. Place a frying pan over a high heat, add oil, and fry the meat until golden brown on both sides. Finish with a large knob of butter and turn the meat a few more times. Add the meat pieces to the vegetables in the oven for approximately 4–5 minutes, remove the meat when the internal temperature is 118 °F / 48 °C, then allow to rest on the cutting board for approximately 5 minutes before serving.

Coarsely chop a little thyme and add, together with the plucked Brussels sprout leaves. Drizzle over olive oil and season with salt and a few turns of the pepper mill. Serve in the ovenproof dish with the sauce on the side, or arrange directly on the plates.

Red wine sauce

Peel the onion and cut into quarters. Place a saucepan over a high heat and add a few drops of oil. Fry the onion and garlic until they are a nice golden-brown color all over.
Pour over the wine and stock and bring to a rolling boil. Skim the sauce, then lower to a medium heat. Add the thyme.
Allow the source to reduce to half the volume (approximately 20 minutes). Sieve, thicken if necessary, and season with salt and pepper.

Memories of Hunting

A roe deer buck with enormous antlers had appeared in the area. He was seen increasingly often during the summer, and more and more of us were keen to gain the kudos of felling such a noble beast. Fall came, and with it the hunting season. Now was the time. All the hunters were ready, myself included. But the end of every day's hunting brought only disappointment. After showing himself right up to the start of the season, he'd suddenly vanished in a puff of smoke. I had completely given up hope when one day at the end of October I was waiting at my stand and the dogs drove a buck out from the forest. And there he was, with his magnificent antlers. But at that speed, in a clearing with a lot of brush, there was no point trying for a shot. I felt the disappointment rising when he came to a sudden stop. I was in the perfect position—and that's how I came to take one of my most long-awaited shots.

—**Hubbe**

Preparation
45 minutes
Cooking
40 minutes
Makes
4 portions

Wallenbergare
14 oz. (400 g) roe venison,
   ground
1½ tsp. salt
2 egg yolks
1½ cups (400 g)
   whipping cream
oil and butter

Herb breadcrumbs
2 oz. (60 g) white bread,
   crusts removed
1 pinch thyme
1 pinch fennel seeds
1 pinch salt

Brown butter
14 tbsp. (200 g) butter

Mashed potato
1½ lb. (700 g) peeled
   potatoes
7 tbsp. (100 g) butter
¾ cup + 4 tsp. (200 ml) milk
salt and white pepper

Accompaniments
lingonberry relish
butter-fried mushrooms
   (optional)

Venison wallenbergare

Wallenbergare *is a Swedish dish generally made with veal, but this recipe using roe venison works really well. You do need a food processor to make it, but it can be of the most basic kind. One tip is to make the mixture and shape the burgers the day before (or at least a few hours before) you intend to serve them. The burgers are much easier to fry when they have come straight from the refrigerator. Here they are served with a little fried mushroom and mashed potato, but I think the most important accompaniment to this dish is the classic lingonberry relish, which provides a contrast to the rich burger and mashed potato. Enjoy!*

Herb breadcrumbs

Blend the ingredients in the food processor until they form crumbs.

Wallenbergare

The mixture works best if you make it from meat that's as freshly ground as possible, and if all the ingredients have come straight out of the refrigerator. You can even put the mixer bowl and blades into the refrigerator before use. Place the ground meat, salt, and egg yolks in the mixer bowl. Begin blending on high speed for a few seconds so the ingredients are well mixed. Begin adding the cream, continuing to blend. Pour in the cream at an even rate—not too fast and not too slow. Otherwise, there is a risk that the cream will curdle and spoil the mixture. If this happens, the mixture will become slightly grainy and will produce a lot of water during cooking. Transfer the mixture to a new bowl and place in the refrigerator.

Line an ovenproof dish with greaseproof paper and sprinkle with breadcrumbs. A cookie cutter the size of a large burger makes a useful tool here. If you have one, place it in lukewarm water together with a large spoon. Shape each burger (weighing approximately 6½ oz. / 185 g) with the wet spoon and one hand, and press into the cookie cutter. Remove the cookie cutter and press out with damp fingers (I usually make burgers ¾ in. (2 cm) deep and 4–5 in. (10–12 cm) in diameter). If you don't have a cookie cutter, make the burgers as round as you can with your hand and the spoon. Sprinkle with breadcrumbs and place in the refrigerator.

Preheat the convection oven to 345 °F (175 °C).

Place a frying pan over a medium heat. Add oil and the burgers. When you fry *wallenbergares*, it's important that you don't fry them too quickly. Turn the burgers carefully and add a good-sized knob of butter. Fry until they are a nice golden brown, then transfer to an ovenproof dish and put the dish on the middle rack of the oven. Bake the burgers for approximately 5 minutes (internal temperature 150 °F / 65 °C). If you bake them for too short a time, they don't fluff up, and if you leave them for too long, they shrink and become dry. Serve with the accompaniments.

Mashed potato

Carefully peel and cook the potatoes. Drain the potatoes when they are cooked and allow the steam to dissipate. Mash the potatoes and add half of the butter. Warm the milk and add to the potatoes, a little at a time. Stir with a whisk or large spoon. Add the remaining butter and stir again. Season with salt and a few turns of freshly ground pepper, if liked.

Brown butter

Melt the butter in a saucepan over a medium heat. Stir with a whisk when it starts to bubble. When the butter changes color to light brown and starts to smell nutty, it's done.

Preparation
10 minutes, if you
have premade the
wallenbergares
Cooking
10 minutes
Makes
4 portions

Sandwich
8 slices rye bread
3 tbsp. butter
2 cold, cooked roe venison
  wallenbergares
  (see page 137)
4 boiled potatoes
roast onion
garden cress, cut

Hot cucumber mayonnaise
4 tbsp. mayonnaise
1 tbsp. Bostongurka
  (pickled cucumber relish)
approx. 2 tsp. sriracha
  hot chili sauce or
  cayenne pepper
salt and black pepper

Sandwich with *wallenbergare*

In the unlikely event that you have a spare wallenbergare *or two, you can make this decadent sandwich. It's perhaps a bit too oozy to take with you on a hunt, but then again sometimes you have to choose taste over practicality. I love to serve this sandwich with hot cucumber mayonnaise, boiled potatoes, and a sprinkle of roast onion on top.*

Hot cucumber mayonnaise

Mix all the ingredients in a bowl. Season and add heat according to taste with sriracha—or cayenne pepper, because if you use too much sriracha the mayonnaise may become too runny.

Sandwich

Slice the burgers and potatoes. Butter the bread and place the slices of potato on four of the slices of bread. Spread the cucumber mayonnaise over the potatoes, and then add the burger slices. Top with roast onion, garden cress, and a final buttered slice of bread. Wrap the sandwiches in plastic film. Greaseproof paper feels more traditional, but unfortunately it rustles too much for sitting in a blind.

Preparation
30 minutes
Cooking
30 minutes
Makes
4 portions

Tartare
5 ½ oz. (150 g) trimmed roe
    venison bottom round
1 shallot
4 slices rye bread
1 tbsp. butter
a few pickled grilled
    tomatoes (see below)
a few pickled chanterelles
    (see right)
olive oil
salt and black pepper

Pickled grilled tomatoes
4–6 green tomatoes
4–6 small red tomatoes
2–3 sprigs tarragon
1 peeled garlic clove
rapeseed oil, olive oil

Pickled chanterelles
11 oz. (300 g) small yellow
    chanterelles
7 tbsp. (100 ml) apple cider
    vinegar
2 tbsp. strong vinegar, 12%
6 tbsp. (90 g) sugar
1 ¼ cups (300 ml) water
2 star anise
2 bay leaves
4 allspice berries

Tarragon mayonnaise
¾ cup + 4 tsp. (200 ml) oil
¾ oz. (20 g) fresh tarragon
1 egg yolk
1 pinch salt
1 tsp. tarragon vinegar or
    white wine vinegar
1 tsp. Dijon mustard
black pepper

Diced tartare of roe venison bottom round

A simple variant on steak tartare using roe venison works well as a snack—or why not as an appetizer? If the latter, assume about 2 oz. (50 g) of meat per person. I sometimes get a real craving for a classic tartare (diced pickled cucumber, capers, onion, Dijon mustard, chopped parsley, and raw egg yolk), and I like to use roe or fallow venison bottom round if I have any in the refrigerator or freezer.

Pickled grilled tomatoes

I think it's a bit much to light the grill just to grill tomatoes, but next time you have green tomatoes to hand and the grill lit, these are well worth the effort. Halve the tomatoes and grill quickly over a high heat. Then dress them in equal parts rapeseed oil and olive oil together with herbs and garlic. Place in the refrigerator until it's time to enjoy them.

Pickled chanterelles

Trim the mushrooms and sear them in a dry frying pan over a medium heat. Place the mushrooms in a well-cleaned glass container or another appropriate container with a tight-fitting lid. Measure out the other ingredients into a saucepan and bring to a rolling boil over a high heat. Pour the brine over the chanterelles and leave to cool. Store in the refrigerator.

Tarragon mayonnaise

Trim the tarragon and pick out the coarsest stalks. Heat the oil to 140 °F (60 °C) in a saucepan over medium heat. Pour the warm oil over the tarragon and blend in a food processor or with a stick blender for approximately 3 minutes. Sieve the oil and leave to cool.

Place the egg yolk in a bowl and add the salt, vinegar, and mustard. Slowly whisk in the oil. If the mayonnaise becomes very thick before all the oil has been used, you can add a few drops of water. Continue until the oil is finished, then season with salt and a little freshly ground black pepper. Store the mayonnaise in the refrigerator.

Tartare

Peel and finely chop the shallot. Slice and dice the meat into very small cubes. Mix the meat with the shallot in a bowl and season with a little olive oil, salt, and pepper.

Slice the bread across the middle and fry in butter on both sides in a frying pan over a medium heat. Arrange the bread on a plate, then the meat, and top with tarragon mayonnaise, chanterelles, and grilled tomatoes.

In Sweden, as well as moose and roe deer, there are also fallow deer, red deer, and reindeer. In a photograph, it can be hard to distinguish a fallow deer from its relative, the red deer, but in reality the red deer is significantly larger and has a shorter tail. Moreover, when the fallow deer's shovel-shaped antlers have developed, these are obviously different from the red deer's more pointed antlers. The fallow deer, which is larger than the roe deer, has the Latin name *Dama dama*.

To quickly distinguish deer species from a distance, you can also study their movement patterns. Red deer appear to float over the terrain while roe dear leap high and long. Fallow deer bounce and jerk stiffly and are well known for their high jumps on straight legs. Unlike red deer, fallow deer are more prone to standing at bay when the dogs are driving—in other words, the deer doesn't continue straight on but turns back and stays within a narrow area.

In Södermanland, there are many fallow deer; in some drives, there can be 50–100 individuals. Here on the farm, we have an enclosure with around 300 individuals.

Fallow deer

The current fallow deer population has existed in Sweden for about 500 years. They are also known to have been in the country long before that but disappeared during the most recent Ice Age. The animals prefer deciduous and mixed forests. Fallow deer don't usually do much damage in the forest, but when they graze in fields and plantations, they can cause harvest losses.

Biology & ecology

Male: buck
Female: doe
Young: fawn

In winter the fallow deer's fur becomes darker, but in summer it is reddish brown with white dots. The population of wild fallow deer is largest in Skåne, in southern Sweden, but they are found all the way to Uppland, halfway up the country. Once they have found a place they like, they usually stay in the area. A buck can weigh up to 310 lb. (140 kg), a doe about half that.

Hunting periods

Fallow deer, all animals: entire Sweden October 1–20 and November 16–February 28.
Antlered animals and fawns: entire Sweden September 1–30, stalking or blind hunting only.
Does and fawns: entire Sweden October 21–November 15 and March 1–31, stalking or blind hunting only.
Hunting of fallow deer can take place from an hour before sunrise to an hour after sunset. During the hour after sunset, only stalking or blind hunting methods may be used.

Types of hunting

Hunting with dog or stalking or blind hunting. In many parts of Sweden, hunts are organized in fallow deer enclosures.

Dogs

Short-legged driving dogs such as the Drever, Dachshund, and Basset Hound.

Weapons

Class 1 rifle or single-barrel shotgun with Brenneke or slug-type ammunition.

Designated targets

Often, you shoot a large proportion of fawns and are more sparing with adult bucks.

A few slivers of fatwood make it easy to light a fire even when it's damp out.

149

Carpaccio
approx. 11 oz. (300 g) fallow
  deer bottom round
½ carrot
3 ½ oz. (100 g) snap peas
3 ½ oz. (100 g) pea shoots
¼ cucumber
1 pot of cilantro
3 ½ oz. (100 g) white shimeji
  or shiitake or
  button mushrooms

Cilantro & lime dip
3 ½ tbsp. (50 ml)
  crème fraîche
3 ½ tbsp. (50 ml) mayonnaise
½ lime
1 tsp. soy sauce
1 tbsp. cilantro, coarsely
  chopped
salt and black pepper

Fallow deer carpaccio

This dish is a little reminiscent of how you make spring rolls, but instead of using rice paper I use thinly sliced bottom round. These fragrant parcels are both fun to make and taste great! Try serving them as a small appetizer or as finger food at a party.

Carpaccio

Trim the bottom round of any sinews and membranes. Slice it into thin slices with a very sharp knife. One tip is to place the bottom round in the freezer for a little while first so it's easier to slice it thinly and evenly.

The length of the vegetable strips should be a little longer than the width of the final meat roll. Peel and slice the carrot into thin strips. Rinse and trim the snap peas and cut into thin strips. Trim the pea shoots. Peel and remove the seeds from the cucumber and cut into thin strips. Chop the cilantro. Trim and, if necessary, halve the mushrooms.

Place the meat slices on a cutting board or a large dish. Arrange the vegetables and mushrooms on top and roll up.

Coriander & lime dip

Squeeze the lime and mix all the ingredients in a bowl. Season with salt and pepper and serve with the rolls.

Preparation
20 minutes
Cooking
30 minutes
Makes
4 portions

Grilled fallow deer hearts
2 fallow deer hearts
rapeseed oil
salt and black pepper

Black pepper gravy
1 shallot
1 cup (250 ml) game stock
1 cup (250 ml) veal stock
2 tbsp. red wine
1 tbsp. black pepper
sherry vinegar
rapeseed oil
salt

Accompaniments
1 piece horseradish
4 egg yolks
fresh French fries
parsley

Grilled fallow deer hearts special

At restaurants where I've worked, we've always called tenderized beef or bottom round with grated horseradish and egg yolk the "Minute Steak Special." When I've looked for the dish online, there doesn't seem to be any particular gastronomic history attached to the name "Special". So let's create one. And try out these accompaniments with a freshly grilled fallow deer heart!

Grilled fallow deer heart

Light the grill. Rinse the hearts in cold water for 1 minute. Dry the hearts with paper towel and place on a cutting board. Cut each heart lengthways into slices approximately ⅓ in. (1 cm) thick. The slices will have holes in, but do your best to make them stay together. Rub the slices with a little oil, then season with salt and pepper. Grill when the coals and the grill are very hot, for about 1 minute per side. Allow the meat to rest for a couple of minutes and then serve with the accompaniments.

Black pepper gravy

Blanch the peppercorns quickly twice to make them a little milder: Bring the water to the boil in two small saucepans. Add the black peppercorns to one saucepan. Leave the peppercorns to boil for a few seconds, then strain off the water and immediately place the peppercorns in the other saucepan. Strain again and lay the peppercorns on paper towels to cool. Allow to dry completely, then blend coarsely in a coffee mill, or place the peppercorns in a tea towel on a cutting board and crush using the handle of a large knife or mallet.

Peel and finely chop the shallot. Fry in a saucepan for a few minutes over a high heat in a few drops of oil, stirring constantly, until it starts to color. Add the ground pepper. Allow to fry for about a further 1 minute. Pour over the wine and stock and bring to a rolling boil. Reduce the heat to low and allow the sauce to reduce to about half (approximately 15–20 minutes). Season with sherry vinegar and salt.

Accompaniments & serving

Peel and grate the horseradish. Top the grilled heart with grated horseradish and make a little hollow in the center for the raw egg yolk. Serve with the black-pepper gravy and fresh French fries tossed in salt and finely chopped parsley.

Memories of Hunting

Few things are as exciting as when Hubbe and I go out to stalk deer. Creeping through the woods in silence takes enormous focus. A misstep that breaks a twig, or too swift a movement, can mean we're spotted by a fallow deer and have to start over. On this particular day, Hubbe was guiding me because we were after a particular deer. We moved slowly through the trees toward a herd of deer out in the field. We wriggled through the vegetation for the last few yards. Slowly, we moved closer. Hubbe pointed out which animal was the target and silently arranged his backpack as a support for my rifle.

That was the first animal I both shot and dealt with right down to the butchering. For the first time, I dressed an animal in the field, opening it and removing all the innards. To be honest, it was more difficult than I'd thought, both in terms of the task and the mental aspect—and I've worked frequently with butchering and dealing with meat. It smells and it's bloody; it's quite simply a very different thing to do, and something you definitely don't encounter in regular, everyday life.

—Micke

Preparation
20 minutes + 4 hours'
marinating
Cooking
1½ hours
Makes
4 portions

Venison shoulder
2¼ lb. (1 kg) boneless
  venison shoulder
1⅓ cups (300 ml) red wine
1 carrot
1 onion
7 oz. (200 g) porcini or
  button mushrooms
3 tbsp. wheat flour
2 tsp. salt
3½ oz. (100 g) smoked
  pork belly, diced
1⅔ cups (400 ml) game
  stock (see page 80)
1⅓ cups (300 ml) water

1 bunch of thyme
2 dried bay leaves
12 small onions
11 oz. (300 g) waxy potatoes,
  washed and halved
  (optional)
rapeseed oil and butter
salt and black pepper

To serve
2 tbsp. flat-leaf parsley,
  coarsely chopped
mashed potatoes
  (see page 137)

Venison shoulder bourguignon

*Probably the best autumn stew in the world, and perfect
to take with you to warm up over the fire for lunch during
a drive hunt. If you do this, you can add a few potatoes to
cook with it over the last half hour. At home, this stew works
best with really buttery mashed potato. Bon appétit!*

Venison shoulder

Trim the shoulder of any sinews and cut into pieces approx-
    imately 1½ in. × 1½ in. (4×4 cm). Place the meat in a bowl and
    pour over the wine. Leave to marinate in the refrigerator
    for at least 4 hours.
Peel and cut the carrot into 1-in. (3-cm) pieces. Peel and chop
    the onion into wedges. Trim and halve the mushrooms.
Remove the meat from the wine (setting the wine to one side).
    Dry the meat, then fry it in equal parts butter and oil in
    a deep cast-iron pan over a high heat, stirring occasionally,
    for approximately 2–3 minutes. Add the carrot, onion,
    mushrooms, and pork belly. Season with salt and sprinkle
    with flour. Fry for 3–4 minutes while stirring. Add the wine
    from the marinade, the stock, and the water. Bring to
    a rolling boil and skim. Add the spices and reduce to a low
    heat. Cover the pan with the lid ajar and allow the stew
    to simmer gently for 30 minutes.

To serve

Peel the onions, halve them, and place in the stew. If you're
    using the potatoes, add them, too, in which case you may
    need to add a little water. Simmer for a further 30 minutes.
Make sure the meat is completely tender, and season with
    salt and pepper. Top with parsley. Serve with mashed
    potato or allow to cool so you can reheat it and serve
    to hungry hunters.

Preparation
20 minutes
Cooking
30 minutes
Makes
4 portions

Hjortskav
1 lb. (500 g) leg of venison,
    thinly sliced
1 onion
3 ½ oz. (100 g) scaly wood
    mushrooms
3 ½ oz. (100 g) sliced bacon
2 tsp. salt
2 tsp. dried thyme
5–6 dried juniper berries,
    crushed
1 tbsp. soy sauce
7 tbsp. (100 ml) water
¾ cup + 4 tsp. (200 ml)
    game stock (see page 80)

1 ¼ cup (300 ml)
    whipping cream
salt and
    black pepper
rapeseed oil
    and butter

To serve
4 tbsp. pickled onions
4 dried crushed juniper
    berries
2 tbsp. finely chopped
    chives
mashed potatoes
    (see page 137)

Hjortskav

A top tip for what you can do with leg meat—a really tasty game dish! Legs are a cut that take up a lot of space if you store them with the bones in. Using thinly sliced leg meat, this is a dish that's quick to cook over the fire in a large pan or griddle.

Hjortskav

Line a freezer container approximately 4×8 in. (10×20 cm) with plastic film. Remove the bone from the leg and pack the meat lengthways in the container. Cover with plastic film and press the meat down well. Put the lid on and freeze.

Remove the meat from the freezer approximately 1 hour before you intend to start cooking. Remove the plastic film and slice the meat thinly while it's still half frozen, with a knife or a slicing machine if you have one.

Peel, halve, and slice the onions. Trim and halve the mushrooms. Cut the bacon into slices approximately 2 in. (5 cm) long.

Fry the meat in a deep cast-iron frying pan or casserole in equal parts butter and oil for 2–3 minutes over a high heat until it starts to turn golden brown. Season with pepper. Add the salt, spices, mushrooms, onion, and bacon. Continue to fry for a further 4–5 minutes while stirring. Add the soy sauce, water, stock, and cream. Bring to a rolling boil, then reduce to a low heat. Cover the pan with the lid ajar and allow the *hjortskav* to simmer for about 20 minutes. Season.

To serve

Serve the *hjortskav* with smooth and buttery mashed potatoes. Top with pickled onions and chives and a few crushed juniper berries on the side.

**Pre-rigor mortis
venison burgers**

Preparation	**Venison burger**	**Dressing**
15 minutes	approx. 1 lb. (500 g) meat	2 tbsp. grainy mustard
Cooking	from a newly shot deer,	2 tbsp. chili sauce
5 minutes	freshly ground	2 tbsp. mayonnaise
Makes	8 slices cheese	
4 portions	rapeseed oil	**Accompaniments**
	approx. 2 tsp. salt	4 hamburger buns
	black pepper	4 tomato slices

Pre-rigor mortis venison burgers

When I worked at Restaurang Djuret, we did a special dinner with Äleby Farm in Sörmland (Södermanland), a county on Sweden's east coast. An experienced hunter had just shot a fallow deer, and we cooked the meat immediately, before rigor mortis had set in. We cooked everything, from the testicles and shoulder to the pink-roast loin of venison and tenderloin served with blood sauce. The evening concluded with a late light supper around the open fire, with burgers made from scraps of leftover meat. I don't think I've ever received so many compliments for a burger. Interestingly, the biggest difference in the meat before and after rigor mortis is noticeable in the ground meat. So, if you ever have the opportunity to take cuts from a newly killed animal, my top tip is to make burgers. They work just as well with moose or roe deer meat.

Venison burger

Light the grill and wait until the coals are ready. Place the ground meat in a bowl and season with a little salt and pepper. Stir, then shape 4 equal-sized hamburgers. Rub a little oil into the burgers, then grill over a high heat on both sides for approximately 2–3 minutes per side. Grill until the internal temperature is 132 °F (56 °C). Finish by adding the cheese on top and allowing it to melt. Serve with the other accompaniments.

Dressing

Mix the mustard, chili sauce, and mayonnaise in a bowl.

Accompaniments

Quickly grill the cut sides of the hamburger buns just before serving. Spread the mayonnaise on the bread, and top with the tomato slices and burgers. Enjoy what's—hopefully—the juiciest burger you've ever eaten!

HARE

Hunting hare with a hound can be really enjoyable, and I find it to be a very relaxing and peaceful hunting method. Hare hunters are almost like a small club of their own within the hunting fraternity. The fact that you can sit down and take it easy in the forest has given it a bit of a reputation as an old man's sport, but not all hunting has to be an adrenaline rush.

You can go out alone or with some friends, and you may find hare tracks, which are especially visible in fresh snow, or you can allow the hound to find a hare. You can sit and grill sausages and the hare will turn up, and you may get a glimpse of it as it bounds past. Because hares often run in laps, it won't be long before it appears again, running in its own tracks. Sometimes it can be an hour before it passes the same place; sometimes it makes a tighter loop and is back in half an hour. It's up to you to decide when you think the dog has run enough and it's time to load your rifle and wait at the stand.

Hares aren't stupid, and they use a range of tricks to distract the dog. For example, they often jump forward then reverse abruptly and backtrack. Then they do a big leap to the side and thus create a scent that suddenly just stops, so that the hound runs into a trail dead end. The hound is completely dumbfounded—just where did the hare go?—and has to start searching in a circle to pick up the scent again. It's difficult to train a hound to do this; it must work it out for itself. Some hounds make a big circle immediately if they have lost the scent, and will pick up the prey, while others find this more difficult.

When you're hunting for field hares, it's best to stay close to roads, gates, bridges across streams, and other points where the terrain narrows, as the hare then has to run through a specific place. Hares are good at losing a hound, for example by diving under a sheep fence and crossing the sheep pasture. The hound comes to the fence, realizes it has to find a hole and then falls far behind.

With hares you don't shoot over more than 100 ft. (30 m), and when the hare has been shot, the dog often gets a bit sulky when it realizes the hare can't run any farther. As a rule, it's a good idea to change place after shooting a hare, because the fresh scents from the shot hare remain and can make it difficult for the hound to know which track to follow. The hare is dressed in the field, and you put a few fir twigs in the abdomen so it stays open and can air out. Then you hang the hare for a couple of days, before skinning and cooking it.

The great thing about hare hunting, apart from being a pleasant day in the forest, is its simplicity. Even if you have good hunting luck and shoot two hares, you just carry them to the tailgate of your vehicle, drive home, and hang them. There isn't the same amount of post-hunt work as with larger game.

Hare

Hares are both fast and smart and can move at up to 45 mph (70 km/h) if they need to escape. The fact that they also hear very well and have sharp sight with a wide angle of vision means they are highly aware of their surroundings and can give the hound a run for its money.

Biology & ecology

Forest and field hares are the same species, but the forest hare is smaller with a shorter tail. The tail of the field hare is longer and black, and the ears are also longer than the forest hare's. The eyes are yellowish brown, unlike the dark red eyes of the forest hare. The forest hare is found across almost the whole of Sweden, while the field hare's range extends as far north as the southern parts of Norrland. Hares are herbivores that eat grass, other low-growing plants, and twigs, and the field hare also likes to eat clover and grain from fields.

Hunting period

Field hare: entire Sweden September 1–February 28.
Forest hare: in southern Sweden September 1–February 15; other parts September 1–February 28.

Types of hunting

Hunting with a driving dog.

Dogs

Hound, Drever, or Dachshund.

Weapons

Class 3 shotgun or rifle.

Designated targets

Forest hares have dwindled in number, and many hunters therefore avoid shooting them even if they get a clear shot.

Preparation
1 hour
Cooking
2 hours
Makes
4 portions

Slow-cooked hare shoulder
2 hare shoulders with bone,
    approx. 1 lb. (500 g)
approx. 2 cups (500 ml) water
1¼ cups (300 ml) game stock
    (see page 80)
1¼ cups (300 ml) red wine
1 onion
2 dried bay leaves
4–5 allspice berries
3–4 cloves
rapeseed oil
salt

Stuffed saddle of hare
1 whole saddle of hare
    with inner fillets,
    approx. 14 oz. (400 g)
approx. 1 oz. (30 g) funnel
    chanterelles
1 shallot
rapeseed oil and butter
approx. 2 tsp. salt
black pepper

Blood sauce
2 cups (500 ml) braising
    liquid from the hare
    shoulders
1 tsp. cornstarch
1 tbsp. Scandinavian dark
    syrup, or light molasses
1 tbsp. cognac
7 tbsp. (100 ml) pig's blood
salt and black pepper

Roasted root vegetables
2 carrots
4 parsnips
1 garlic clove
3½ oz. (100 g) leaf spinach
olive oil and butter
salt

Hare in blood sauce

*Here I've deboned the saddle so the loin fillets hang together.
This requires a hare with sufficient fat and membranes.
Otherwise, you can cut out the loin fillets separately and snip
a small cut in the middle of each of them to make space
for the mushroom filling.*

Slow-cooked hare shoulder

Fry the shoulders in a little olive oil in a high-sided cast-iron
    pan for approximately 2 minutes per side over a medium
    heat. Season with salt and add the water, stock, and wine.
    Bring to a rolling boil and skim. Reduce to a low heat. Peel
    and halve the onion. Add the onion and spices. Allow the
    stew to simmer with the lid on but ajar for approximately
    1½ hours. Check it from time to time and add a little water
    if the liquid isn't covering the meat. Check to make sure the
    meat is completely tender. Sieve and set the liquid to one
    side. Place the shoulders on a cutting board to cool a little.
    Remove the bone and any sinews from the meat and cut
    into pieces approximately 1×1 in. (3×3 cm).

Stuffed saddle of hare

Preheat the convection oven to 210 °F (100 °C).

Trim the mushrooms and peel and finely chop the shallot. Melt a knob of butter in a frying pan over a medium heat and sweat the mushrooms and shallot for approximately 3 minutes while stirring. Season with plenty of salt and allow the mushrooms to cool on paper towel.

Trim any sinews on the inner fillets from the saddle of hare. Place the fillets in a food processor together with a little salt and quickly blend the meat, approximately 30 seconds. Place the ground meat in a bowl and mix the mushrooms into it. Set aside in the refrigerator.

Divide the mushroom filling as evenly as possible and place in the middle of the loin fillets. Roll the fillets up and fix with plastic film. Place in an ovenproof dish and bake on the middle rack of the oven for about 30 minutes, until the internal temperature is 107 °F (42 °C). Remove from the oven and remove the plastic film. Fry the fillets in a frying pan over medium heat in equal parts butter and oil. Season with salt and pepper. Fry the fillets until the internal temperature is 118 °F (48 °C). Leave to stand for at least 5 minutes before serving.

Roasted root vegetables

Preheat the convection oven to 430 °F (220 °C).

Peel and coarsely chop the carrot and parsnip. Place everything in an ovenproof dish with a lightly crushed garlic clove. Drizzle over olive oil and add a knob of butter. Season with salt and pepper and roast on the middle rack of the oven for approximately 25 minutes. Shake the dish from time to time. Remove the dish from the oven and check that the vegetables are soft. Mix in the spinach and season with salt and pepper.

Blood sauce

Pour the braising liquid from the shoulders into a saucepan and bring to the boil. Reduce to a medium heat. Mix the cornstarch with a little cold water and stir into the liquid in the saucepan. Add the syrup or molasses and reduce to a low heat, then simmer for approximately 10 minutes. Turn off the hob, then add the cognac and blood, stirring carefully. Sieve the sauce and season with salt and pepper. Don't let the sauce boil as it will curdle. Add the cubed shoulder and heat carefully, then serve with the stuffed saddle and other accompaniments.

Hare

BIRDS

A successful day in the field. The pigeons are alert, so remember to stay in cover as they fly in.

The ideal place and time for hunting wood pigeons is in a pea field in late summer. The peas have matured, and there's a good chance of an exciting wood pigeon hunt. You use decoys—models of wood pigeons—which you set out in the field. There are different ideas about how best to deploy the decoys to attract the wood pigeons to land among their plastic friends. You can put them in a v-shape or a u-shape or use decoys with moving wings, and so on. Once the pigeons have become curious about the decoys, they are within firing range for the hunter in the hide.

The hide can be a rigged camouflage net in a ditch, or you can be in a bush or hidden by trees. Wood pigeons are very alert. One tip is to cover your face, because it really stands out among the greenery. Nor should you stare at the birds as they are about to fly in, but instead squint out from under your eyebrows so you don't turn your whole face toward the sky before it's time to shoot. It's quite difficult shooting, because pigeons fly much faster than you think, so you'll have to swing your weapon well ahead of them. The difference between actual bird hunting and clay pigeon shooting is that the living bird increases and decreases its speed in ways that a clay pigeon doesn't. It's also difficult to judge the distance against the sky, and generally you overshoot. You just have to stay cool and wait for them. If you've fired at

Hunting birds is as much fun for the master as it is for the dog. A good retriever makes a great hunting companion.

a bird but it doesn't appear to have been hit, try shooting again if you have a double barrel. It's quite likely that one or more of the pellets will strike home. The bird will then die anyway, but it will take much longer. I hang the shot pigeons for a couple of days before dressing them.

A dog is used to retrieve shot birds, as they can be very difficult to find if they fall into the forest. If you shoot the bird 65 ft. (20 m) above your head, it can continue well away from your location, simply through inertia.

Duck hunting is another enjoyable type of hunt. Perhaps the best variety is to hunt wild ducks, which at dusk come into lakes and bays after spending the day out on the sea. It often feels like it's too dark to see any birds at all when you stand there waiting, but birds stand out quite well against the sky in the little remaining light. As is usual in bird hunting, you fire upward at a minimum of 45 degrees to avoid the risk of hitting anyone.

My own favorite bird to hunt is the ptarmigan. It isn't something you hunt to fill the freezer, as it doesn't produce a lot of food, but the activity itself is very enjoyable. I hunt ptarmigan with a German Shorthaired Pointer in the birch forest below the mountain slope. Of course, there are also ptarmigan above the tree line, but it can be very windy up there, so I mainly hunt in the borderland between the mountain and the birch forest, often in the Arjeplog range in the area around Miekak, in Swedish Lapland. I've been hunting there for many years, and I think it is an incredibly beautiful place.

To succeed at ptarmigan hunting, you need a smart dog with a good level of fitness—walking in the mountains is demanding. Even as the hunter, you'll realize that you're walking long distances over rough terrain and that you're constantly moving up and down the mountain slopes. The more you move, the greater the reward will be. If you walk along a path or trail, you won't shoot many ptarmigan; you simply have to go out into the terrain.

To hunt ptarmigan and other forest birds in Sweden, you need a hunting permit for state land. The land is divided into squares on the map. There's often a bag limit—that is, a limit to how many ptarmigan and grouse you can shoot per day.

The dog should wear a bell around its neck and a vest so you can see where it is. To begin the hunt, you release the dog. It's usually easiest to get out when the ground is still slightly damp with dew. Then the dog will get the scent of the birds more easily than if it's dry. If it's dry and windy, there will be less scent from the ptarmigan. In dry years, the ptarmigan are happy to stick to streams and around lakes where there are a lot of berries, but if there has been a lot of rain they will be a little higher up. The most important thing is to walk toward the wind so the dog can scent the ptarmigan clearly. It's a good idea to let the dog rest from time to time, and you should also have good rations with you. Take the opportunity to analyze the situation and remember that you're doing both your dog and yourself a favor by resting instead of just carrying on. A tired dog blunders more easily and scares away the ptarmigan once it has their scent.

If you hunt ptarmigan in the mountains in the early fall, you should wear ankle-height boots. I think tall boots get too sweaty, and if you wear a stable ankle-height boot you reduce the risk of twisting your ankle, which isn't fun to do far out on the mountain with poor cell phone coverage. If there's snow on the ground, you'll need skis and a white snow suit. One interesting thing about ptarmigan is how well they sense the coming weather: If you're hunting in the winter, you'll sometimes notice that the ptarmigan have gathered on tree branches, looking like small snowballs. This is usually a clear sign of impending snowfall; they seem to know when they need to eat plenty before the bad weather comes. Sometimes you run into a grouse, and that's really fun. In general, you are so surprised you don't have time to shoot.

Birds	In Sweden, some 30 different species of wild birds are hunted, of which pigeons and ptarmigan are among the most common.
Biology & ecology	Mallards are highly adaptable and are therefore found in many, sometimes urban, environments. The wood pigeon, too, lives in a wide range of locations, except for the mountains. With ptarmigan, on the other hand, we find ourselves in mountain environments and the Nordic forest. Willow ptarmigan and rock ptarmigan are similar and can be difficult to distinguish.
Hunting periods	Mallard: In most parts of Sweden August 21–December 31. Mallard may be hunted from an hour before sunrise to an hour after sunset. Willow ptarmigan and rock ptarmigan: Dalarna County, Jämtland County, Västerbotten County, and Norrbotten County August 25–February 15. Wood pigeon: Dalarna County, Gävleborg County, Västernorrland County, Jämtland County, Västerbotten County, and Norrbotten County August 1–December 31. Other parts of the country August 16–December 31.
Types of hunting	Retrieving dog breeds.
Weapons	Class 4 shotgun or rifle.
Designated targets	The hunting of birds is regulated just like any other type of hunting. Some birds, such as mallard ducks, are to a large extent released into nature purely for hunting.

Preparation
20 minutes
Cooking
20 minutes
Makes
2 portions

Fried pigeon breast
4 pigeon breasts
butter

Curry & garlic oil
1 garlic clove
1 tbsp. rapeseed oil
3 tsp. curry powder
1 tbsp. brown butter
1 tbsp. olive oil
salt and black pepper

Curry-fried vegetables
1 yellow zucchini
1 green zucchini
½ cauliflower
salt and black pepper

Pea & curry sauce
1 onion
1 green apple
1 tbsp. curry powder
7 tbsp. (100 ml) white wine
¾ cup + 4 tsp. (200 ml)
  chicken stock
7 tbsp. (100 ml) milk
7 tbsp. (100 ml) whipping
  cream
5 tbsp. (70 g) peas
1 tbsp. squeezed lemon juice
2 tbsp. butter
salt and black pepper

Fried pigeon breast

The inspiration for this dish came from chicken curry. Because the pigeons had been attracted to a field of peas, it felt like freshly picked peas were the right accompaniment. In this recipe, I've plucked the birds to retain the skin. Wood pigeons don't have very thick skin, but it's always worth plucking the feathers by hand instead of simply cutting out the breast meat. It both protects the meat and gives a little extra flavor to the dish. See the plucking process as a moment of relaxation.

Fried pigeon breast

Fry the pigeon breasts, skin side down, in butter in a frying pan over a medium heat. Season with salt and pepper. Fry the skin side for about 2 minutes, then reduce the heat to low and turn the breasts over. Fry for a further 2 minutes. The meat should have an internal temperature of 120 °F (48 °C) degrees. Lift the breasts out of the frying pan and allow to rest for a few minutes before serving. Cut each breast into 2 or 3 pieces and serve with the other accompaniments.

Curry & garlic oil

Peel the garlic and grate it finely into a small saucepan. Add rapeseed oil and curry powder and fry slowly for about 1 minute while stirring over a low heat. Remove from the heat, then season with salt and pepper. Add the warm brown butter and olive oil.

Curry-fried vegetables

Rinse and trim the zucchini. Using a mandoline or sharp knife, cut long, thin strips from a quarter of the green and yellow zucchini. Set aside in the refrigerator for serving. Cut the remaining zucchini into approximately ¾-in. (2-cm) cubes.

Rinse and trim the cauliflower, and pick out the florets. Cut the florets into pieces as uniformly sized as possible. Fry the cauliflower florets in the curry and garlic oil in a frying pan over a medium heat for 2–3 minutes, stirring from time to time. Add the zucchini cubes and fry for a further 2–3 minutes. Season with salt and pepper.

Top the fried zucchini and cauliflower with the raw zucchini strips.

Pea & curry sauce

Peel and finely chop the shallot. Peel and finely cube the apple. Fry the onion and apple in butter in a saucepan over a medium heat for about 1 minute while stirring. Add the curry powder and fry for a further 1 minute. Pour over the wine, stock, milk, and cream, and bring to the boil. Reduce to a low heat and simmer for 15–20 minutes.

Add the peas and allow to simmer for a minute or two. Blend the sauce until smooth. Season with lemon juice, salt, and pepper, and serve with the pigeon and other accompaniments.

On the breast side, you need to be extra careful. Pluck a few feathers at a time. If you get too eager, you can easily make holes in the skin. This is best done outdoors, as there are a lot of feathers.

Preparation
30 minutes
Cooking
20 minutes
Makes
2 portions

Whole roast willow ptarmigan
2 whole, plucked willow
    ptarmigans
12 sprigs thyme
4 sprigs rosemary
4 sprigs tarragon
2 tbsp. butter
salt
twine

**Onions cooked in
beer & angelica**
2 onions
¾ cup + 4 tsp. (200 ml)
    pale ale
1 tsp. fresh or dried
    angelica seeds
7 oz. (200 g) boiled
    sliced potatoes
2 tbsp. butter

Whole roast willow ptarmigan

In general, what goes with what in cooking is highly logical. Going by the rule of serving the ingredient with what's in season right then, or what the game itself has eaten, may sound clichéd and pretentious, but it's never wrong. People are often unsure about what goes with game, and I always turn the question around and ask them to list things that don't go together. There aren't usually many. So it's quite simple: You only exclude flavors you don't like yourself.

I've created a recipe using willow ptarmigan based on exactly that rule. I picked some angelica from the mountain path, and we'd brought some potatoes, beer, and onions to the hunting camp. Simple, but perhaps the tastiest recipe I've ever created.

Whole roast willow ptarmigan

Stuff the ptarmigan with the herbs and bind the thigh bones together with twine. Fry the birds carefully on all sides in butter in a frying pan over a medium heat. Using a spatula or spoon try to protect the breast so the thighs are cooked to a higher temperature. The breast should be cooked to an internal temperature of 120 °F (50 °C), and the thighs can be cooked to 140 °F (60 °C). Allow the ptarmigan to rest for a few minutes and serve with the accompaniments.

Onions cooked in beer & angelica

Peel and slice the onions into thin slices. Fry in butter in a frying pan over a high heat for 3–4 minutes, stirring continuously. Add the angelica and beer. Reduce to medium heat and allow to cook gently for a couple of minutes. Add the potatoes and season with salt. Serve with the whole roast ptarmigans.

Preparation
40 minutes
Cooking
40 minutes
Makes
4 portions

Mallard breast
8 duck breasts with skin
butter
salt

Butternut squash
14 oz. (400 g)
   butternut squash
2 tbsp. + 1 tbsp. butter
7 tbsp. (100 ml)
   game stock (see page 80)
salt

Truffle gravy
1 shallot
1⅔ cup (400 ml) game stock
   (see page 80)
2 tbsp. Madeira
2 tbsp. truffle, chopped
sherry vinegar
rapeseed oil
salt and black pepper

Accompaniments
2 heads red Belgian endive
approx. 8 Brussels sprouts
olive oil
salt

Mallard breast with truffle gravy

Early in my career, I learned how endive enhances the flavor of truffles. In this recipe I've used the leaves raw, but if you've never eaten it before I recommend that you try serving the endive fried and perhaps poached in Madeira and truffle gravy. Regardless, there's a great combination of the sweetness from the butternut squash, the truffle gravy, and the flavorful wild duck breast.

Mallard breast

Fry the duck breasts in butter in a frying pan over a medium heat. Fry both sides, season with salt, and cook until the internal temperature is 115–118 °F (46–48 °C). Remove the breasts from the pan and allow to rest for at least 5 minutes before serving (final temperature 126–129 °F / 52–54 °C). Slice the breasts or serve them whole.

Butternut squash

Remove the skin and seeds from the squash. Cut half of the squash into smaller pieces, approximately ¾ × ¾ in. (2×2 cm), for the puree, and the remaining half into larger pieces approx. 1½ × 1½ (4×4 cm) for roasting.

Heat 2 tbsp. of butter over a medium heat in a saucepan. Add the smaller pieces of squash, stir, and season with salt. Fry for a few minutes, stirring constantly, until they start to develop a golden-brown color. Pour over the stock, reduce the heat to low and put the lid on the saucepan. Allowed to continue cooking over a low heat for a further 10 minutes. Mash with a fork or wooden spoon, then season.

Fry the large pieces of squash in 1 tbsp. of butter in a pan over a medium heat. Make sure they are nicely colored on every side, add salt then reduce the heat to low. Cook the pieces for approximately 5 minutes, until they are just soft right through.

Truffle gravy

Peel and finely chop the shallot. Fry until golden brown in a little oil in a saucepan over a high heat, stirring constantly. Pour over the Madeira and allow it to cook into the shallot. Add the stock and bring to the boil. Reduce the temperature to low and allow the sauce to simmer for about 20 minutes. Finish by adding the truffle and seasoning with a couple of splashes of sherry vinegar, salt, and pepper.

Accompaniments & serving

Trim and remove the leaves from the endive and Brussels sprouts. Place the leaves in a bowl and season with a little olive oil and salt. Stir again. Serve the duck breast with the squash, truffle gravy, endive, and Brussels sprouts.

Memories of Hunting

My best memory of bird hunting is definitely of a ptarmigan hunt in the mountains of Arjeplog, in Swedish Lapland. It was an early fall day, not too hot. My friend and I both had dogs, and we were hunting through the beech forest near Sartajokka. We saw birds everywhere. I was on a roll when, suddenly, I heard a whirring noise: There were two capercaillies in the air, and bang, bang, I'd shot a double. It wasn't long before I'd got a bead on another capercaillie. Three capercaillies and several ptarmigans on the same day in this environment... I was the world's happiest hunter! I've never experienced anything like it either before or since. Once I'd carried those 44 lb. (20 kg) of game birds home, I was probably the world's tiredest hunter, too.

—Hubbe

Preparation
30 minutes + 6 hours'
  brining
Cooking
3 hours
Makes
2 portions or 4 portions
as an appetizer

Confit
4 mallard thighs with skin,
  approx. 11 oz. (300 g)
1 tsp. salt
1¼ cups (300 ml) duck fat
1 garlic clove
2 sprigs thyme

Cauliflower cream
11 oz. (300 g) cauliflower
7 tbsp. (100 ml) milk
¾ cup + 4 tsp. (200 ml)
  whipping cream
salt

Roasted parsnips
3 parsnips
11 oz. (300 g) Savoy cabbage
2 ½ oz. (70 g) dried apricots
1 tbsp. flat-leaf parsley,
  coarsely chopped
butter and olive oil
parsley

Confit mallard thighs

When I worked at The Square in London in the early 2000s, we often served sautéed Savoy cabbage and dried apricots as a garnish for game birds. It's an accompaniment that I've taken with me and used in several of the restaurants I've worked at since then.

Confit

Place the thighs in an ovenproof dish with the skin side down. Sprinkle the salt over the meat, cover with plastic film, and allow to brine in the refrigerator for at least 6 hours.
Preheat the convection oven to 210 °F (100 °C). Add the duck fat, crushed garlic clove, and thyme stalks to the thighs and bake in the center of the oven for 2–3 hours. Lift out a thigh and check that the meat is completely tender. Sieve the fat and save in the refrigerator for next time.
Fry the thigh with the skin side downward in a knob of butter.

Cauliflower cream

Trim the cauliflower and cut it into smallish pieces. Bring the milk, cream, and cauliflower to the boil in a saucepan. Reduce to a low heat. Simmer for about 15 minutes, stirring from time to time, until the cauliflower is completely soft. Remove from the heat and blend until smooth. Season with salt.

Roasted parsnips

Preheat the oven to 390 °F (200 °C). Peel the parsnip and cut into 1–1½ in. (3–4 cm) pieces. Place them in an ovenproof dish with a little butter and olive oil. Roast on the middle rack of the oven for approximately 10 minutes. Trim and shred the Savoy cabbage. Add the cabbage to the ovenproof dish, stir and add salt, and cook for a further 5 minutes. Coarsely chop the apricots. Check that the parsnips and cabbage are soft. Add the apricots and parsley. Season with salt. Serve with the confit mallard thigh and the cauliflower cream.

195

Recipe Index

Wild game can be a sustainable, environmentally friendly, and healthy alternative to farmed meat. We offer *The Wild Game Cookbook* as an insight into hunting and, especially, for ways to bring out the rich flavors of wild game.

Be it as a hunter or as a chef, please always check the current regulations and hunting seasons in your area. We encourage people to mind the provenance of their game meat: wild and local are best.

Also note that in certain areas some species in this book may be unavailable—or that they may be protected, even endangered. In these cases, the recipes can be easily adapted and will hopefully provide inspiration for other meals.